T0318903

Scientists and Poets #Resist

Personal/Public Scholarship

VOLUME 5

Series Editor

Patricia Leavy (*USA*)

Editorial Board

Scope

The *Personal/Public Scholarship* book series values: (1) public scholarship (scholarship that is accessible to academic and popular audiences), and (2) interconnections between the personal and public in all areas of cultural, social, economic and political life. We publish textbooks, monographs and anthologies (original material only).

Please consult www.patricialeavy.com for submission requirements (click the book series tab).

The titles published in this series are listed at *brill.com/pepu*

Scientists and Poets #Resist

Edited by

Sandra L. Faulkner and Andrea England

BRILL

SENSE

LEIDEN | BOSTON

Cover image: *Stars of Eger*, by Paul Bilger

All chapters in this book have undergone peer review.

Library of Congress Cataloging-in-Publication Data

Names: Faulkner, Sandra L., editor. | England, Andrea, editor.
Title: Scientists and poets #resist / edited by Sandra L. Faulkner and
  Andrea England.
Description: Leiden ; Boston : Brill Sense, 2020. | Series: Personal/public
  scholarship, 25429671 ; volume 5 | Includes bibliographical references.
Identifiers: LCCN 2019041710 (print) | LCCN 2019041711 (ebook) | ISBN
  9789004418806 (paperback) | ISBN 9789004418813 (hardback) | ISBN
  9789004418820 (ebook)
Subjects: LCSH: American literature--21st century. |
  Science--Language--Literary collections. |
  Technology--Language--Literary collections. | Freedom of speech. |
  Government publications--Censorship--United States.
Classification: LCC PS509.S3 S35 2020 (print) | LCC PS509.S3 (ebook) |
  DDC 808.108/3581--dc2 3
LC record available at https://lccn.loc.gov/2019041710
LC ebook record available at https://lccn.loc.gov/2019041711

ISSN 2542-9671
ISBN 978-90-04-41880-6 (paperback)
ISBN 978-90-04-41881-3 (hardback)
ISBN 978-90-04-41882-0 (e-book)

'evidence-based' and 'science-based') and not only *say* them, not only *write* them, but *use* them—to theorize, hypothesize, narrate and imagine. To #Resist the forces that would separate us from each other's knowledge, expertise and understanding. The richly textured work in these pages, written by poets and scientists, sometimes collaboratively, evokes a painful moment in our national story, but creates within that moment a space of possibility. They remind us that we need to start somewhere in order to get anywhere. In 'Notes from Indiana: The Crossroads of America, 2018,' Charnell Peters writes: 'I will start here / with the grit under my fingernails / the eyelash on my friend's cheek / the beads in my cousins' hair / the pale silks of July's sweet corn / my god what shall I make?' A charge within a charge: where will *you* start, and what will *you* make? This is an important book and I'm glad we have it."
– Sheila Squillante, Director, MFA Program in Creative Writing and assistant professor of English at Chatham University

"When the Trump administration banned the use of seven words in HHS documents—words pointedly related to gender, abortion access, and science—they went beyond merely trying to frame a public discussion according to their own agenda: it is one thing to identify preferred language, and quite another to forbid, legally, the use of words with which one doesn't agree. But Truth, as Flannery O'Connor once put it, 'does not change according to our ability to stomach it.' The poems, stories, and essays in this anthology demonstrate, openly and often painfully, the day-to-day necessity of the words this administration seeks to suppress. This is a crucial, courageous book."
– Philip Memmer, author of *Pantheon*

This work is for all of the scientists, poets, and dreamers who #Resist

CONTENTS

Acknowledgements   xiii

Science-Based Vulnerability   xv

Part 1: It Begins with Our Words...

1. It Begins with Our Words   3
   Daniela Elza

2. Rescue the Words   13
   Norma C. Wilson

3. Evidence-Based   15
   Jane Piirto

4. Notes from Indiana: The Crossroads of America, 2018   17
   Charnell Peters

5. Late Term   19
   Jessica Smartt Gullion

6. Before Roe vs. Wade   27
   Sarah Brown Weitzman

7. The Double Helix Is Not Two-Faced, It Is an Embrace   29
   Elizabyth A. Hiscox

8. That Light Bill   31
   Samantha Schaefer

Part 2: #Resist

9. Kidnapping Children and Calves (of a Tender Age)   35
   Lee Beavington

10. What Does Transgender Look Like?   43
    Shalen Lowell

11. Woman with PCOS Lingers on the Possibilities of Science   45
Minadora Macheret

12. Half a Schroedinger   47
Karen L. Frank

13. Bubbles   49
Kris Harrington

14. The Ease and Difficulty of Hating and Loving One's Self   53
Franklin K. R. Cline

15. Seven Thoughts about Butterflies   55
Ben Paulus

16. It Takes a Village   57
Michelle Bonczek Evory

17. The Capital of Failure   59
Scott M. Bade

Part 3: Evidence

18. Field Notes & Marginalia   63
Sandy Feinstein and Bryan Shawn Wang

19. =   73
Terri Witek

20. America, My America   75
Sarah Brown Weitzman

21. Expressive Writing Paradigm: An Experiment in Righting   77
Jessica Moore

22. To Beat the Banned   79
Scott Wiggerman

23. Four Years   81
Jennifer K. Sweeney

24. While the Offering Stales in the Calm   83
Mark Kerstetter

25. Photosynthesis   85
     Susan Cohen

Questions and Activities for Further Discussion   87

Notes on Contributors   91

ACKNOWLEDGEMENTS

The cover image, *Stars of Eger*, was created by Dr. Paul Bilger.

We thank Erin Elizabeth Smith, Director of SAFTA (Sundress Academy for the Arts) for our residencies, which facilitated our meeting and the realization of this project.

We thank Patricia Leavy, Series Editor for Brill Sense's series *Personal/Public Scholarship*, for choosing to work with us on this volume and for putting out the call for work addressing the banned words and censorship. Sandra is grateful for Patricia's friendship and general kick-butt feminist approach to the world. Here is a feminist fist-bump for you!

We also want to thank John Bennett, Acquisitions Editor at Brill Sense, for seeing value in this project. Jolanda Karada, Production Coordinator at Brill Sense, kept us on track with the important details and helped produce this gorgeous book. Thank you!

And finally, we thank, Paul Chambers, in Marketing and Sales at Brill Sense for getting this volume in readers' hands. We hope you all enjoy it.

SCIENCE-BASED VULNERABILITY

This volume of creative nonfiction, personal narrative, and poetry is a conversation between poets and scientists and a dialogue between art and science. The authors are poets, scientists, and poet-scientists who use the seven words—"vulnerable," "entitlement," "diversity," "transgender," "fetus," "evidence-based" and "science-based"—banned by the Trump administration in official Health and Human Service documents in December 2017 in their contributions. The contributors use the seven words to discuss their work, reactions to their work, and the creative environment in which they work. The resulting collection is an act of resistance, a political commentary, a conversation between scientists and poets, and a dialogue of collective voices using banned words as a rallying cry—*Scientists and Poets #Resist*—a warning that censorship is an issue connecting us all, an issue requiring a collective aesthetic response.

The editors and contributors approached this project from a place of **vulnerability**, using their experiences as poets and scientists in a time of censorship and attack to speak from a place of susceptibility to harm. The speaking of those experiences turned **vulnerable** into a show of strength and solidarity.

Andrea England: I first met Sandra during a writing residency at SAFTA (Sundress Academy for the Arts; http://www.sundresspublications.com/safta/) in late Winter 2017. Little did either of us expect to make such a strong personal and political connection, or imagine that shortly before we met Donald Trump would become our next President. Later that year, we met again in residency at SAFTA. This was soon after the CDC (Centers for Disease Control) received a list of words from the Trump administration that they were not to use in communications and/or official documents. These words were: *entitlement, evidence-based, transgender, fetus, diversity, vulnerable, and science-based*. I immediately wrote a sestina utilizing six of these, and it was then that Sandra and I decided that these words deserved a larger context in which to evolve and be understood.

BANNED SESTINA

I remember you when you were just a **fetus**
All fibula and forehead, turned to **diversity**,
keeping your sex a secret part of in utero **entitlement**.
Now you've got Serenity, once Samuel, **transgendered**.
She's got your back on the bus with her **vulnerable**
weave. Even my freshmen know research is **evidence-based**.

Where do I find it? How do I cite **science-based**
examples? Doctors weren't worried when you were a **fetus**
They said you'd either sink or swim. I was the **vulnerable**
one. My students appropriate, misuse **diversity**
in sentences about Jesus and race, the T in **Transgender**.
Transvestite one laughs in her slim jeaned **entitlement**.

Online students give it up, this sixth sense of **entitlement**!
SHTSTE. Please keep to the five; they're **evidence-based**
like the anatomy of experience or natal **transgender**.
Oh how I waxed and took baths when you were a **fetus**,
the sweat running swell in my wild-life **diversity**:
endangered white rhino, sandwich—**vulnerable**

to Papa John's teeth. Papa don't preach **vulnerable**
because men are told their born to **entitlement**
my father, your father, don't marry into **diversity**.
Therapists assign books that are **evidence-based**.
Divorce rates don't help the plight of the **fetus**.
Would you rather your baby be gay or **transgender**?

Which of these matter, which syntax, **transgender**?
Regardless the period, the colon, our end wanes **vulnerable**
as the torn labrum, labia, ice packs for that **fetus**.
Graduate? Two pair of shoes? Please admit your **entitlement**
like a tree admits its roots. Math is **science-based**
a day added or subtracted. It admits its **diversity**;

the story problem of conception: that **diversity**.
My doctor misbelieved your sex. **Transgendered**?

No, head circumference, weight…**evidence-based**
or mystery? Choice or genes, as **vulnerable**
as the next, except for a parent's **entitlement**.
I've made many choices. I too, was a **fetus**,

an **evidence-based**, fraternal, twin: **vulnerable**
and fated to **diversity** and loss. Even hope is **transgender**—
Tricky, **entitled**. Our (your) very freedom, a hothouse **fetus**.

Sandra L. Faulkner: When I first met Andrea at SAFTA in February 2017, we fell into dialogue about life and work as if we had known one another for years, as if we had been roommates in college, as if we were long time collaborators and friends. I talked about being a social scientist who uses poetry in her work as feminist practice and research methodology (see Faulkner, 2018, 2020). Andrea talked about the creation of poems as reflective of personal experience and connection to tradition, how teaching was the distillation of creative practice. We sat at SAFTA's kitchen table writing, talking, grading, and eating fresh eggs we gathered mornings from the chickens and ducks up the hill from our perches on either side of the table. Because of our connection, we arranged to be at SAFTA the same week the following December.

At the beginning of that week, we took a drive in Andrea's car in the neighborhood surrounding SAFTA and ended up finding the put-in dock for a local lake. We conceived this project there in Andrea's parked car, the heated seats a bougie comfort as we ate chocolate truffles, talked about poetry and politics, relationships and language, Andrea writing with pen in a notebook, me pecking out ideas in my MacBook, looking into and past the water outside of the car. I started a sestina that didn't work out. Andrea started and finished one that did work as you see above.

When we returned to our everyday lives, I saw a call for book proposals that dealt with resisting the CDC banned words in some manner. The post-script from series editor, Patricia Leavy, resonated with me and mirrored the conversations that Andrea and I had been having about the power of poetry:

> Fascists always go after our words. Words are powerful. Words are disruptive. Words are dangerous. Let's show them just how powerful our words are. Let's use these words and others words to create an intellectual and artistic militia. Let's out-create the destruction around us.

This outlet seemed the right venue for realizing the ideas we had been discussing. We wanted to honor my identity as a social scientist AND a poet and Andrea's appreciation for science AND poetry. We wanted to use the power of poetry and science, the lenses of logos and pathos.

Andrea and I were happy to receive a contract for *Scientists and Poets #Resist* and thrilled with the array of work that poets and scientists sent us, how they engaged with language as poets do, how poet-scientists used the process of creativity and **vulnerability** to resist censorship, rescue, and reimagine the words. Mark Kerstetter speaks of the importance of being vulnerable in "While the Offering Stales in the Calm." "The very possibility of becoming someone viable requires **vulnerability**. Yours. Mine." Franklin K. R. Cline also speaks of the strength of being **vulnerable** in "The Ease and Difficulty of Hating and Loving Oneself."

//maybe instead of morose I mean **vulnerable**

not sure what the difference is or
if they inform each other

if they talk to each other the way the fly
talks to the screen as it yearns to talk to the trees

Other contributors note the importance of speaking out and acting for those most **vulnerable** in our society. Kris Harrington writes in "Bubbles," "And like so many of my peers, I mostly direct my energy outward into saying what I have to say, into raising awareness through words and demonstrations, into speaking up for the **vulnerable** among us." And Lee Beavington writes of being triggered by Rachel Maddox's tears when she reported on immigration policies and separating children from their parents in tender-age facilities in the essay, "Kidnapping Children and Calves of a Tender Age." Beavington makes an explicit connection between teaching biology labs that use fetal bovine serum (FBS), which is extracted from the hearts of fetal calves in slaughterhouses, and separating small children from their parents in detention centers in the US.

Without relationship, there is less capacity for empathy. Remember Rachel Maddow's on-air tears: she inspires our path toward compassion. And so I cry for each child kidnapped from their parents. I cry for each fetal calf whose heart is sucked dry every 20 seconds of every day to fulfill our scientific duty. I cry for the fetal calf whose heart I gave away to my students.

Our work expands the scope of other art resistance projects, such as *The CDC Poetry Project* (https://cdcpoetry.wordpress.com/about/), which is an online space for poetry using the seven banned words, and the edited collection *Poetic Inquiry as Social Justice and Political Response* (Faulkner & Cloud, 2019). We expand such work by focusing on the connections between artists and scientists. For instance, Elizabyth A. Hiscox sent us, "The Double Helix," wherein she discusses her upbringing as focused on BOTH science and religion.

> My mother: the daughter of a Methodist minister, the daughter of a nuclear physicist.//
> My childhood was of her grand design: angels and angles were both important.
> Hypotenuse and Gabriel sat on equal footing: bringing different, good news.

Daniela Elza opens her essay, "It Begins with Our Words," with the **evidence-based** statement:

> It's not surprising that when fundamentalist and totalitarian regimes come into power the first thing they go after is language. Our poets, scientists, journalists, artists, and intellectuals have always been in danger under such governments, often dying for their words alone. These regimes can only work if they control the narrative.

This anthology is a way for artists *and* scientists to control the narrative, because as Norma Wilson pleads: "Help! A ban on the right to choose one's words/ blocks health, human services and a poet's work." Wilson reclaims the banned words in the lines of a sestina. "The less we think for ourselves, the more he'll gain." The poets and scientists we present in this collection all reclaim the words, many with a sense of anger and urgency, showing that art and science are precisely the tools we need in repressive times. Pearl Jam reminds us in their song, "I Am Mine," that "I only own my mind." The contributors in this collection embody this as they ask important questions like Sarah Brown Weitzman in *America, My America*:

> America, I will always love you
> but who are you? the land?
> the people? the government?
> the leaders? the laws?
> If I had to choose I would say

the land and the laws
though I once thought thunder
a thing of wonder until I heard
the **scientific explanation**.

I have been asking myself similar questions the past two years as I react to headlines, each one more outrageous then the previous one. I started a series of resistance poems that I call, *Trigger Warning*, that enact and reflect my feminist rage, and let me work through my feelings about the politics of privilege and a Trump presidency these past few years like Jennifer K. Sweeney does in "Four Years."

The first acts are of negation. Policies, people, empty offices that will never be full. Words can be sheared away. ***Diversity*** and ***vulnerable***. Gone are the facts, the **evidence**, **science** swept from sites with a silent click. Entitled in his Palm Beach White House, he erases ***entitlement***.

***

TRIGGER WARNING[1]

"If there were an armed guard inside the temple, they would have been able to stop them," the President suggested. "Maybe there would have been nobody killed except for him, frankly."—After the Tree of Life Synagogue Massacre, Pittsburgh, October 27, 2018

Sisters, lock your truck
and the hunting weapon of feminist rage,
find the bullets in the kitchen drawer:

A fear of guns is symbolic of what?

I do not own any guns   own (m)any guns
not even a gun
being stolen right in your driveway:

If Abortion stops a beating **fetus**
what does a gun stop?

The moment my brother loaded an air-gun with rock salt,
not bothering to refer to me by name,
and shot my bare summer:

   When did this begin?

My **entitled** student once called me *commie snowflake feminazi*
and then **vulnerable,** repeated, *shot gun.*
Treat them with much respect:

   Did this begin?

Their dead names morphed into prayers
and purses with gun holders,
glove boxes with thoughts:

   Why can't you see me?

A loaded gun in your driveway
bullets in the kitchen drawer.

   You see me?

I dream of AK57s in a line around the bathroom stall
in my daughter's school, bodies tossed over playground fences-
evidence based on a shot through your stall door:

   If someone shoots, will there be **Science** class?

I remember this on a loop for years:
Repeated shot gun
being stolen right in your driveway.

   What if I buy a lifetime membership in the NRA?

We love our guns.   Your guns.
This shoots on a loop for years.

***

Poets and scientists are not binary in their pursuits; however, they both occupy spaces that have been interrogated and misunderstood for centuries. Allison Hawthorne Deming speaks to the historical and traditional stance of the public concerning scientists and poets, "We are made to embody the mythic split in western civilization between the head and the heart." Yet both poetry and science seek to contain chaos through form, and through experimentation and manipulation, to arrive at new (and often complex) understandings or solutions to the conundrums and idiosyncrasies that plague our ever-evolving environment. This "environment" spans the physical, chemical, and sociopolitical landscape, and encourages, if not demands, an interdiscourse between poets and scientists. The result of this interdiscourse and the hope of this anthology, which mingles the words of poets and scientists, is to locate a communal voice in which to address the current and worrisome ideologies that are the product of our current governing body.

To bodies then! The poet Alberto Rios poses, "Science may be our best way of understanding the world, / But it may not be our best way of living in it." If we can collectively commit to the idea that the mind and the body not only require each other to survive and evolve, but complement each other in ways that can improve our daily politics and personal interactions, we might arrive at something like this:

> Remember photosynthesis?
> Soon, some will insist we
> just call it magic so we forget
> how life depends on light.

These lines from Susan Cohen's poem, "Photosynthesis," illustrate the danger of binaries in our current political makeup and highlight this dilemma in terms of censorship. This poem forces us to choose between "photosynthesis" and "magic," "life" and light." What happens when words become extinct? In the context of this poem, life ceases to exist. A profound moment also occurs earlier in the poem, when the reader encounters the catch and release of what it means to define and/or ignore the spectrum of human discovery and being as, "This poem is **transgender**, meaning, / surface is one thing, but essence / another." In our age of technological advancement, where marriages and leaders can rise or fall on the drop of an emoji or a few misplaced words, we must come to acknowledge that both "surface" and "essence" are needed to sustain our relationships, our economy, and our country.

Both scientists and poets use a creative process in their work. The idea that there is a scientific method divorced from the creative process or that writing poetry does not ever mean the use of logic is a false binary. Sandy Feinstein and Bryan Wang demonstrate how this is a false dialectic in their essay "In Field Notes and Marginalia." Feinstein and Wang interweave how understandings of science help one understand and experience literature and vice versa.

If science provides the surface, it is surely the poet who eeks out and communicates its essence. Scott Bade, in his poem, "The Capital of Failure," admits the condition of blame that is deep seeded in our culture, "Surely there is more than one ailment bound up in failure." The speaker goes on to confess, "When I play the guitar, failure sings / its greatest hits." No more than any other time in history do we need to address, resist and re-address the ways in which we see, speak, and define our failures towards progress. This is the work and the spoils of true resistance, an interdiscourse where we can entertain both science, and the music it insists upon.

NOTE

[1] "Trigger Warning" by Sandra L. Faulkner first appeared in *Glass: A Journal of Poetry*. Poets Respond (May 31, 2019). Copyright Sandra L. Faulkner. http://www.glass-poetry.com/poets-resist/faulkner-trigger.html?fbclid=IwAR3JVcKmPfL32WSTixwnvt6EI93ke1MkryxcHgh55Y8dRzoxVX8d7he_0bY

REFERENCES

Deming, A. H. (1998). Science and poetry: A view from the divide, 11. *Creative Nonfiction, 11*. Retrieved from https://www.creativenonfiction.org/online-reading/poetry-and-science-view-divide.

Faulkner, S. L. (2018). Crank up the feminism: Poetic inquiry as feminist methodology. *Humanities, 7*(3), 85. https://doi.org/10.3390/h7030085

Faulkner, S. L. (2020). *Poetic inquiry: Craft, method, and practice* (2nd ed.). New York, NY: Routledge.

Faulkner, S. L., & Cloud, A. (Eds.). (2019). *Poetic inquiry as social justice and political response*. Wilmington, DE: Vernon Press.

Ríos, A. (2009). The leukemia girls. *The dangerous shirt* (p. 42). Port Townsend, WA: Copper Canyon Press.

PART 1

IT BEGINS WITH OUR WORDS...

DANIELA ELZA

1. IT BEGINS WITH OUR WORDS

It's not surprising that when fundamentalist and totalitarian regimes come into power the first thing they go after is language. Our poets, scientists, journalists, artists, and intellectuals have always been in danger under such governments, often dying for their words alone. These regimes can only work if they control the narrative.

There are many dark periods in Bulgarian history, not the least disturbing of which is when thousands from the intelligentsia disappeared without a trace. In Bulgaria, the poets, the writers, and intellectuals were often also the revolutionaries. After the September uprising in 1923, deemed to be the first antifascist uprising, poet Geo Milev writes the epic long poem *September*. It describes the bloody, uneven battle between the well-armed and trained government army and the poorly armed workers and peasants. It speaks of the horrors, the sacrifices, and the bravery of a people who rose up to fight against oppression. The poem makes the government squirm, and they sentence Geo Milev, barely 30 years old, to a year in prison. The next day he is called into the police station for a small "clarification," from which he never returns. Decades later his skull, with its glass eye, is found in a mass grave near Sofia. He lost his eye on the front lines, but lost his life for writing a poem.

As much as I want to think of this as something of the past, attacks on books and words, and the untimely deaths of writers and revolutionaries, are still plaguing us. In 2007 a car bomb exploded on al-Mutanabbi Street in Baghdad—the historic center of Baghdad bookselling. Dozens lost their lives and at least a hundred were injured. It mobilized us writers to respond with *Al-Mutanabbi Street Starts Here*, an anthology of poetry by the same name. In 2014 the poetry community mourned Arab-Iranian poet Hashem Shaabani, executed by the order of Iranian President Hassan Rouhani. Hashem fought for human rights and was sentenced to death under the charge that he is "waging war on God" (Harriet Staff, 2014). The mind boggling purge that began in 2016 under the reign of Turkish President Erdoğan has affected the justice system, education, government employees, the military, police and media. "According to the P24 press freedom group, there are more than 160 journalists behind bars in Turkey, most of whom were arrested under the state of emergency imposed after the coup attempt" (Wintour, 2018). As I write this Jamal Khashoggi, a prominent Saudi journalist and columnist for the Washington Post, has been missing for over two weeks. It's presumed he was assassinated in the Saudi Arabia embassy in Turkey, while trying to sort out paperwork for his marriage. A critic of the regime, he left his country when he knew it wasn't safe for him to do his work there. Books matter. Words matter. That is why they are a threat to such regimes. They throw the proverbial monkey wrench in their story.

We live at a time where **entitlement** trumps **diversity,** when "truth" is a self-serving convenience, a time when government can create "alternative" facts to serves their cause. It's a world where **evidence-based** and **science-based** narratives compete with money, conspiracy theories, extremist cults and views, where corporate-serving narratives are manufactured on a whim. Inconvenient books and stories can be banned or burned. Inconvenient people and whistleblowers are punished or worse dispensed with. People argue over easily provable facts. We seem to have left the age of information, and walked straight into the age of misinformation, we now call *post truth*. Many of us are still in the age of how-is-this-even-possible. It's not just possible, it has happened before.

In an article in *The New York Times* Jason Stanley (2016) speaks of how:

> The goal of totalitarian propaganda is to sketch out a consistent system that is simple to grasp, one that both constructs and simultaneously provides an explanation for grievances against various out-groups. It is openly intended to distort reality, partly as an expression of the leader's power. Its open distortion of reality is both its greatest strength and greatest weakness. (para. 7)

Does that sound painfully familiar? We upgrade our computer software regularly, but don't take much care of our delicate mental software. It's hard to deny that we're gullible and susceptible to manipulation, especially given the right conditions of indignity, poverty, or incentive. We live in spaces that are increasingly surveilled, and monitored. If your world is manufactured, then your truth can be too. It's then a stone's throw from there to limit yourself to a group of people who only think like you. Should we be surprised then that "alternative" narratives have moved in from the fringes, and have been sweeping across the US like the wild fires last summer? No, we should not be surprised. It has happened before. We are shocked anew at how fragile democracy can be.

For decades the US has been solving uncompromising financial crises by finding someone to blame, and going to war seems to have been the way it deals with its economic problems. That seems to appease the markets, and the people. For a little while. If you produce weapons, you have to have markets to sell them. If there's no need, you create one by starting a war somewhere. This is the simple logic of supply and demand, profits and being only accountable to shareholders. How is a system like that threatened? The truth can be that monkey wrench thrown in its workings, which makes it sputter, stall, and sow doubt. But today we see multiple narratives, a lot of money behind some of them, and more wrenches in the air.

In an article published in 2013 on *Ceasefire,* Andrew Robinson (2013) discusses Walter Benjamin's analysis of the effects of economic crisis on everyday life in Germany. Robinson (2013) writes:

> [C]apitalism is in crisis because it can't get people to consume as much as it can produce, usually because people aren't being paid enough. As a result, people are left unemployed and machines and factories are left idle. People who adhere to this theory see the Second World War as a resolution of the crisis of overproduction. The state artificially inflated demand by producing weapons. It then destroyed a lot of other resources by using them. This got people producing again, and was a way out of the crisis. (para. 19)

One thing that neoliberalism has had a hard time facing is that its ideology and politics can lead to fascism. We currently see these tendencies played out in a different guise. There is no challenge from the government to property structure, and there is the spectacle that channels people's emotions. "According to Benjamin, fascism inevitably leads to war. War is the only way to channel mass movements and intense emotions, without challenging the property system." But to go to war you need to have a bullet proof story. Or at least one that is immune to monkey wrenches. In the Bush Junior years, we witnessed how it's not easy to find the right lies, or the right metaphors to fire up a nation to go to war. But after a few tries and a whole lot of lies they did. The world cannot afford this kind of brute and ignorant problem solving.

When we read a novel, or watch a play, it creates a reality in which the actions of the characters make sense. The writer has to be consistent to gain the reader's trust. The reader has to suspend disbelief in order to participate fully. That's the contract we enter when we read fiction for the sake of art, entertainment, or to relate it to our lives. When we do that in politics it is problematic. In advertising we are clear what underlies the ad, we know we are being told a "story" for the purpose of being sold a thing. That is why advertising to children is so insidious and is banned in countries like Sweden. Studies show that children are unable to separate the actual program from the commercials shown in between segments. I did not grow up with commercials, and felt that dissonance first hand. My brain tries to integrate the first few frames of the commercial, before it switches gears and recognizes it's a commercial. When it comes to government propaganda it is mostly not clear what kind of contract we enter. And when lies are not a deterrent then you can present any narrative to assert your power. Our storied minds delight in what makes sense to us, what is consistent, and what orders, and simplifies the world to make it more bearable. Capitalism gone global through the multinational corporation is a hard story to sell, because it is a ghost story (Arundhati Roy, 2014); it takes a big machine to create it, and it takes a lot of suspending of disbelief to buy it. There is enough dissonance, and enough people willing to spin a narrative tailored to the ruling administration. And we have some who are willing to say the emperor is naked. We forget there is a big money machine underpinning this propaganda.

Felipe Fernandez-Armesto says in his book *Truth: A history and a guide for the perplexed*: "There is no social order without trust, and no trust without truth or, at least, agreed truth finding procedures" (p. 3). What happens to our mental health, to our communities, and even families, when we're bombarded with bits of contradictory information, when competing narratives pull us in different directions? Is this our latest version of the tower of Babel? In a world dissociated from the world, you can push hate, and manufactured worlds, like cheap street drugs. What we take to be true, what we believe, and what we perceive, have fragile and tenuous threads. Each can influence the other. And each can shift depending on the environment. That becomes easier if you make the real world unbearable. "When people stop believing in something, they do not believe in nothing; they believe in anything" (Felipe Fernandez-Armesto, 1998, p. 3). We forget too quickly what has already happened, because even our memory is compromised in our screen infested immediate gratification reality. But also we forget that authoritarian rhetoric attempts to "convey power by defining reality. The reality they offer is very simple. It is offered with the goal of switching voters' value systems to the authoritarian value system of the leader" (Stanley, 2016). Often that includes creating an enemy of the people and creating fear.

To add to the complexity, and madness, social media reinforces this narrowing, these echo-chambers. We keep thinking of artificial intelligence as something romantic and sexy, but the unpredicted outcomes of algorithms, let loose, sometimes without human oversight, are already running our lives and altering our very soft brain-software. People we disagree with, who challenge us, whose views do not align with ours, are a click away from being unfriended, dispensed with, blocked. Social media mobs and trolls can reduce you to a label in record time, can drag you through the hate-speech dirt (under the guise of *free speech*, of course), can virtually crucify you. It's hard to go down the trash chute of people's opinions. It breeds fear to speak your mind. God forbid if you are **transgender**, or visibly different in skin color, or religion, or you are a group that is used as a tool to create fear and labelled *the enemy of the people*. If you live in an echo chamber, you'll become an echo chamber. This isn't just old and boring, it's dangerous. And we are witnessing more and more the kind of dangerous it is.

Thankfully, people know when enough is enough. In 1968, in the iconic riots in Paris, students at the University of Nanterre and the Sorbonne stood up for their rights and began a revolution that moved beyond its initial demands. More importantly, they opened up spaces for conversations that couldn't be had before. It became necessary to find common ground between students and administration, workers and government. Community isn't just something we feel we need, it's a powerful survival mechanism, it's a place of sanity and humanity. It's good for us to be **vulnerable** with each other, to trust each other, and count on each other. It's good for our brains. What despotic, tyrannical, and totalitarian regimes are after is to splinter that trust in order to control us better. They ritualize violence until it makes sense. They make a spectacle out of it. These aren't new developments. Yet, many of us are still curled up in the **fetus** phase of *how-is-this-even-possible*. Knowing all this, I keep saying to myself, anytime now I'll find out this is some black comedy, a farce, a theatre of the absurd I can go home from, but it isn't.

In 1990 I was a student in a Master's Program in English Philology. We occupied Sofia University and demanded the resignation of then newly elected Petar Mladenov. Even though Mladenov helped topple the totalitarian ruler Todor Zhivkov, it seemed like he continued with the same old politics. After he was caught on camera saying that he'll bring in the tanks against the tens of thousands of anti-government demonstrators (demanding the Communist Party give up its monopoly on power) the students asked for his resignation. I remember being in a chanting crowd so closely packed, my body swayed when the crowd swayed. We were one organism, moving

7

in unison. A cardboard tank, erected in the courtyard of the university, symbolized what Mladenov at first denied he had said. More importantly, we demanded democratic change. The occupation of the university went on for at least a month. It felt more like six weeks. But memory is fickle, so I had to look it up. The support we got was more than inspiring. There were lectures and discussions with visiting experts. Artists and theatre actors came to show their support with performances, and talks. Professors camped out in solidarity with the students. People brought us food, and handed it to us through the bars in the courtyard fence. Eventually, our demands were met. In other parts of the world students haven't been as lucky.

When corporate and political corruption begins to weigh unbearably on citizens, something has to give in. Political shake ups in Bulgaria seem to come about through actions by optimistic, fed up youth looking into the muzzle of their impoverished future. The power of places of knowledge cannot be undermined, they usually are at the head of change and revolutions. That is why they are also the first to be targeted.

Earlier this year (Fagenson, 2018) in the US, survivors of the high school shooting in Parkland, Florida, led the *March for our Lives* demanding gun control. They were dis-regarded, dismissed by the Trump administration, whose policies have the pungent and sickening odor of neoliberalism. This, of course, is a foreboding sign for the government. It doesn't help that the warped and compromised nature of Fox "News" goes to unconscionable lengths to pollute the airwaves, and poison susceptible minds. Then there was the synagogue shooting in Pittsburg, Pennsylvania. My Facebook wall again turned into a long lament of grief, dismay, disbelief, of how-is-this-even-possible.

The US has come to the edge of its hyper-capitalist greed, a neoliberal agenda gone haywire, an agenda that cannot face the consequences of its beliefs and actions. Where money is god, even the god of religion is subservient to the money god. Does it feel like they are now shaking hands and making deals under the table? You can bring your gun to church. You can get a discount on Wednesdays for bringing your conceal and carry permit for a pistol at *Just the Cook* houseboat restaurant in St. Andrews, Florida. It is easier to get a gun than a hot lunch at school. We cannot afford anymore to think the market is wise, or that capitalism has any ethical or social justice concerns. Its bottom line is profit. We also cannot afford to think that this is some act of god. It isn't. The idea of a government calling for less government seems to be a paradox in itself. It is a government which no longer serves the people, but serves some chosen people. Adam Smith's invisible hand is no longer invisible. It is a meddling greedy hand that keeps adjusting the dials to please shareholders. Remember the military industrial complex?

There is only so much you can push a system on people before it reveals its terrible flaws, the many ways it has devised of impoverishing its citizens, its communities, by tampering with their food and water, language and culture, land and environment. Too much is invested in the same old ways, and the system and old institutions hold tooth, claw, and nail. It creates schizophrenic narratives to defend those investments at any cost. If people turned off the TV and started talking to each other, their communities will be better off, their local governments will not be so gutted and impotent.

What happens to trust in times like these? "There is no social order without trust, and no trust without truth or, at least, agreed truth finding procedures" (Fernandez-Armesto, 1998, p. 3). *Greed* and *agreed upon* truth aren't going to make friends under the current ideology because it has to tell itself lies to keep going, or exclude obvious facts in order to sustain its premises.

A much longer time ago Plato did an analysis of different types of governments. In *The Republic* he juxtaposes *fortune* and *virtue in* an oligarchy: "the more they think of making a fortune, the less they think of virtue; for when riches and virtue are placed together in the scales of the balance, the one always rises as the other falls" (Book VIII, p. 210). Plato goes on to talk about what happens when wealth is the main qualification for the job, as if he predicted the Trump government. "Just think what happens if pilots were to be chosen according to their property, and a poor man were refused permission to steer, even though he were a better pilot?" The defects of a system like that are blatantly obvious, still the US elected a brand name for a president (one of poor character and temper), and just confirmed a "judge" of questionable character and morals to a position for life in their supreme court. How do we balance the scales? Plato is not a prophet giving us prophecies, he just thought deeply about human nature, and its propensities. In Book VIII of *The Republic* Plato discusses the transition from democracy to tyranny, as if it's as natural and inevitable a process as the seasons changing.

It's also paradoxical to want certain rights and freedoms while denying them to another group of people. We get George Orwell's *Animal Farm* all over again. We cannot but draw parallels to his *1984* science-fiction dystopian novel with the *doublethink* and *newspeak*. The Greek rhetorician, Isocrates,[1] saw the pitfalls of taking freedom irresponsibly: democracy is not insolence, liberty is not lawlessness, equality is not impudence of speech, and happiness is not a license to do what you please. Yet, we see how these have flared under the encouragement of an amoral government. None of this is new to the world, yet we act like it's unheard of.

In Canada only recently have we began to deal with the shameful episode of residential schools, and recognize that we live on Unceded Aboriginal Territories. It was 2014 when, finally, our city council unanimously voted to formally acknowledge this fact, and gaping oversight. It reads:

> Underlying all other truths spoken during the Year of Reconciliation is the truth that the modern city of Vancouver was founded on the traditional territories of the Musqueam, Squamish and Tsleil-Waututh First Nations and that these territories were never ceded through treaty, war or surrender.

The world moves forward however, and, if history teaches us anything, sooner or later, enough people see through the propaganda and the fabricated narratives, the strategy of *altering and controlling your reality*, sooner or later citizens will stand up in enough numbers, and their voices will be hard to ignore. And it begins with our words. To summon what the inimitable Ursula K. Le Guin said in her speech at the National Book Awards (2014):

> We live in capitalism, its power seems inescapable—but then, so did the divine right of kings. Any human power can be resisted and changed by human beings. Resistance and change often begin in art. Very often in our art, the art of words. (para. 5)

So when a government today begins to control language, especially if that person, or group, is in position of power, there's no time to waste, we cannot afford to not pay attention. Especially if you live in a country where *free speech* is still flaunted as a right, you not only have to take responsibility for what comes out of your mouth, but for what cannot. It's time to fight for your right to keep that right.

Ursula is no longer with us, but her words are. So are Geo Milev's words, and Hashem Shaabani's words, and the thousands of others who have stood up for humanity and freedom, and fought in the service of human rights and dignity. Sooner or later the scales will have to be balanced. Any government worth its salt should take heed, or start preparing for its own demise.

NOTE

[1]   Those who directed the state in the time of Solon and Cleisthenes did not establish a polity which…trained the citizens in such fashion that they looked upon insolence as democracy, lawlessness as liberty, impudence of speech as equality, and license to do what they pleased

as happiness, but rather a polity which detested and punished such men and by so doing made all the citizens better and wiser (Areopagiticus, 7.20 (Norlin)).

REFERENCES

Bulgarian Leader Quits Under Student Pressure. *The Washington Post*. Retrieved from https://www.washingtonpost.com/archive/politics/1990/07/07/bulgarian-leader-quits-under-student-pressure/86c320bb-fe39-43cf-a1d5-00a1d380145f/?utm_term=.09d9651833de

Fagenson, Z. (2018, May 18). "DO SOMETHING," Parkland Survivors urge action after Texas school shooting. *Reuters*. Retrieved from https://www.reuters.com/article/us-texas-shooting-parkland/do-something-parkland-survivors-urge-action-after-texas-school-shooting-idUSKCN1IJ2LU

Fernandez-Armesto, F. (1998). *Truth: A history and a guide to the perplexed*. London: Black Swan Books. (Bantam Press edition published in 1997)

Harriet Staff. (2014, February 6). Iranian poet and activist Hashem Shaabani Executed. *Poetry Foundation*. Retrieved from https://www.poetryfoundation.org/harriet/2014/02/iranian-poet-and-activist-hashem-shaabani-executed

Le Guin, U. K. (2014, November 20). *Books aren't just commodities: Speech at national book awards*. Retrieved from https://www.theguardian.com/books/2014/nov/20/ursula-k-le-guin-national-book-awards-speech

Meiszner, P. (2014, June 25). City of Vancouver formally declares city is on unceded Aboriginal territory. *Global News*. Retrieved from https://globalnews.ca/news/1416321/city-of-vancouver-formally-declares-city-is-on-unceded-aborginal-territory/

Plato. (2000). *Plato's the republic* (B. Jowett, Trans.). Mineola, NY: Dover Publications.

Robinson, A. (2013, August 14). Walter Benjamin: Fascism and Crisis. *Ceasefire*. Retrieved from https://ceasefiremagazine.co.uk/walter-benjamin-fascism-crisis/

Roy, A. (2014). *Capitalism: A ghost story*. Chicago, IL: Haymarket Books.

Stanley, J. (2016, November 4). Beyond lying: Donald Trump's authoritarian reality. *The New York Times*. Retrieved from https://www.nytimes.com/2016/11/05/opinion/beyond-lying-donald-trumps-authoritarian-reality.html

Wintour, P. (2018, May 15). Erdoğan ends UK state visit by calling jailed journalists 'terrorists.' *The Guardian*. Retrieved from https://www.theguardian.com/world/2018/may/15/recep-tayyip-erdogan-theresa-may-uk-state-visit-jailed-journalists-terrorists

NORMA C. WILSON

2. RESCUE THE WORDS

Help! A ban on the right to choose one's words
blocks health, human services and a poet's work
Yet, that ban fits the tweeting pattern of Trump.
Banning "**fetus**," Trump feels entitled to erase
anything he wants the voters to not think.
The less we think for ourselves, the more he'll gain.

Will those who'd ban "abortion" elect him again?
Trump doesn't like three or four syllable words,
banned "**evidence-based**," substitutes fake think.
Consulting with Europe is too much work.
Trump thinks female heads of state should be erased,
denies that Putin's hacking benefitted Trump.

He proclaims, "It's a witch hunt." Yes, Trump
is the witch. From his bargain, what do we gain?
Russian meddling threatens to erase
our voting rights. "**Diversity**'s" banned,
for Trump has no regard for the lives and work
of immigrants. When will the voters think

about all the problems he's causing? I think
we're all endangered by the regime of Trump.
Will his and Putin's conspiracy work?
Democracy's loss is oligarchy's gain.
"**Transgender**," time to speak the banned word.
We'll take to the streets—our voices won't be erased.

Science-based education Trump tries to erase
by countering reason with failure to think.
Kept ignorant, "vulnerable" is the word

© KONINKLIJKE BRILL NV, LEIDEN, 2020 | DOI:10.1163/9789004418820_002

for voters who fall prey again to Trump.
Electing people of conscience, we can regain
control, but this requires a lot of work.

That's the way our democracy works.
I'll put my shoulder to the wheel, I'll not erase
those words Trump banned. Please join me, regain
the time as a poet to write and think
about things more important than Trump.
We'll restore poetic "justice," that's the word,

work together to rescue the banned words,
never letting Trump erase our **diversity**,
we'll invest in everyone's gain.

JANE PIIRTO

3. EVIDENCE-BASED

The Study showed the practice worked with kids.
(Though no one tried it with kids to compare.)
The textbook companies put out their bids.
Lessons, activities, it's "in the air."
"Brain-based," "grit," "mindful," "MI," "checkmark grids,"
theories their gurus spoke to share:
the crowds believed, the bosses popped their lids.

But then professors and researchers began.
They used control groups, wrote big grants
to check the findings that The Study scanned.
The **evidence-based** claim was too scant,
the practice waned. Some new/old master plans
arose, new experts' claims: new times, new rants.

© KONINKLIJKE BRILL NV, LEIDEN, 2020 | DOI:10.1163/9789004418820_003

CHARNELL PETERS

4. NOTES FROM INDIANA: THE CROSSROADS OF AMERICA, 2018

let me be a sinner in the hands of a **transgender** god. / they tell me not to be great again but to transform / over / to be transformed / once more / over / not by taking anything back from invisible forces / or from the visible but unnamed / not by heaping bodies into mountains / and calling them the ends of ourselves / or a beginning / they say I am / I am / I am / worth the claiming / that I can name what is mine / my world / my people / my love / my body / my womb / my breath / every breath its own mountain. / they say we are made in their image. / we too can create / and I will start here / with the grit under my fingernails / the eyelash on my friend's cheek / the beads in my cousins' hair / the pale silks of July's sweet corn / my god what shall I make? / from the rust of my granddaddy's suitcase buckle / and the spikes of the white pine / and gravel from the grocery's parking lot? / a golem / of sorts made entirely in the crossroads of America / my god / Robert Johnson said / I went to the crossroads / fell down on my knees / what invisible and unnamed forces / hover here over bodies / like mine / and unlike / and my god / not just bodies. / it must be something / to make the art here / to pursue the **science- / based** here / where utility is slim and mechanical and holy / my god / what is it to create / within the dust / of the cornfields / the kinds of meanings we can feel / and the ones we can touch. / both tell us what the mourning dove means / every morning / my god, once / I was a **fetus** / and once I became a person / who could make one / and every morning / I am / I am / I am / a Black woman in the crossroads / of America / and everything can be unmade / even states / like fear

© KONINKLIJKE BRILL NV, LEIDEN, 2020 | DOI:10.1163/9789004418820_004

JESSICA SMARTT GULLION

5. LATE TERM

Shortly after my daughter was born, I learned that a woman who came to the health department clinic where I worked was pregnant with a **fetus** that did not have a brain. The best course of treatment for her was a late term abortion; however, because of the politics surrounding late term abortion, along with the fact that she was a Medicaid patient, her doctor could not find anyone to perform the procedure. In addition, the anomaly classified her pregnancy as high risk, and she could no longer be treated at our clinic. I've often wondered what happened to her. In this piece, I juxtapose my own experiences with pregnancy with a fictionalized account of what her experience might have been like.

***

"There's the skull. The spinal column." The tech drew her hand along the string of pearls at the bottom of the screen. My eyes adjusted to the green and black alien vision, sorting the blurred images into a baby.

"Do you want to know the sex?"

I nodded.

She pointed. "There's the labia. She's perfect."

I didn't predict the wrenching sob that escaped my lips. My daughter. My perfect, beautiful daughter.

The sonogram technician printed photos of her for me.

***

The tech ran the wand over Amelia's swollen belly, and Amelia watched the screen, hungry for a look at her baby.

"¿Que ves?" Amelia asked. "Está todo bien?"

*I don't speak Spanish," the tech said. She raised her voice and leaned closer. "No comprendo." She turned to the terminal, frowning and taking measurements of the **fetus**. Photographs spilled from the printer.*

"Take these to your doctor," the tech said, louder than necessary. She did not make eye contact. Amelia clutched the photos and tried to make sense of them.

***

My coworkers stopped working when I came in.

"So?" Sarah smiled.

My eyes watered. "It's a girl!"

We all squealed in delight.

"Awww, a little girl!" Sandra said.

"She's going to be so cute," said Linda.

"A boy and a girl. You have the perfect family," Melicia said.

"I'm so happy for you!" Betsy added.

They all nodded and hugged me. I showed them the sonogram photos amid chatter about dresses and hair bows and my insistence that sex doesn't determine gender but yes all that girly stuff is really cute. We accomplished little work the rest of the day. At lunch we went shopping and I bought a tiny pair of pink striped socks.

***

Amelia sat on the exam table, naked in a blue paper gown that would not close around her form. She held her sonogram pictures in her hands and tried again to make out the shapes. "Dulce Bebe," she said.

The doctor entered the room without a knock, startling her. A translator followed him in.

"Hello, Amelia," the doctor said. "How are you today?"

"¿Cómo estás?" the translator said.

"Todo parece bien. Estoy teniendo muchos problemas con la acidez estomacal. Fui y me hice la ecografía. Me dijeron que te los entregara. ¿Puedes decirme si es un niño o una niña?"

"She had a sonogram," the translator told the doctor.

The doctor took the photos. As he looked through them his smile faded. "I need to make a call to the radiologist," he said. He placed his hand on Amelia's shoulder. "Hang in there. I will be right back."

"Él estará de vuelta," the translator said. She followed the doctor out of the room.

Amelia shivered and rubbed her belly.

***

"What about Madeline?" I said. "We could call her Maddy for short."

"I like that." My husband said.

"I like Isobel too. From that Björk song. It's about this mythical creature that bursts into the forest from a flame." I rubbed my hands across my belly. "What's your name, baby?" I watched a wave of movement from her.

My son toddled over to where we sat on the couch. He lifted his starfish hands to my body. "Belly belly belly," he said. He laughed and walked over to Greg, lifted Greg's shirt and shook his belly. "Belly belly belly."

"I guess I need to lose some weight," Greg said, comparing his gut to mine. He scooped up our son. "Are you calling me fat?" They both laughed like this was the funniest thing ever.

***

"Here, you can have my seat," a skinny man with neck tattoos stood up and gestured to her. Amelia sat down and the crowded bus lurched forward. She watched the world pass by her window, the sunlight glittering on the industrial buildings, the fast food restaurants, the big box stores.

The baby kicked.

She struggled to reconcile this: How can a baby kick if it doesn't have a brain? Is the baby alive or dead?

*"Your body is keeping the **fetus** alive," the translator told her. "When it is born, it will die."*

He kicked again. This can't be right, Amelia thought.

What the doctor told Amelia:

*Your **fetus** does not have a brain or spinal cord. It's a condition called anencephaly. This is likely due to a folic acid deficiency in your body. You should have started prenatal care much earlier. Ideally, we like for women who are trying to get pregnant to start taking prenatal vitamins to prevent this sort of thing. But that's neither here nor there. You are seven months pregnant. You can carry the **fetus** to term, at which time it will die. It would be better and safer for you to have a late-term abortion.*

The trouble is finding someone to do it. You are now considered a high risk pregnancy. Here at the health department, we are not allowed to see high risk women. You need to find a new doctor who specializes in this, and then see if you can find someone to do the abortion. Of course your Medicaid is not going to pay for that, so you will have to get one out of pocket. You're looking at a few thousand dollars for that, and you will have to drive to Dallas. No one in this area will touch something like that. I'm so sorry, Amelia.

What Amelia heard:

Your baby is dead and because you couldn't keep your baby alive you no longer have a doctor.

***

My friends had filled the room with pink and white balloons. Presents spilled over the gift table.

"Oh, you guys, you shouldn't have gone to all this trouble!" I said. Another table had a taco bar and a cake stand that held two dozen vanilla cupcakes with iridescent pink frosting.

"I even hand shredded all that cheese," Betsy said. "Because we love you. And pre-shredded cheese tastes gross."

I hugged her. The room filled with people. We stuffed our bellies with tacos and cupcakes and my friends made us play silly games like how big is Jessica's belly (circumference in inches) and name that baby food (Melicia won when she guessed turkey and yams). I opened gift after gift. Dresses in miniature. A crocheted cap. Receiving blankets. Diapers. More tiny dresses, and socks, and crib-safe stuffed animals, and onsies with appliques of animals and dolls and one with trains.

"She has more clothes than I do," I laughed.

I took the balloons home to my son. He called them "boonas" and he played with them all evening. My husband helped me put the gifts in her bedroom. We ate leftover cupcakes after dinner.

***

"Mama, there is something wrong with the baby," Amelia said to her mother in Spanish.

"What do you mean, something wrong?"

"The doctor says that he is going to die when he is born." Amelia's eyes filled with tears.

Her mother sat in stillness.

"Mama?"

"These white doctors don't know anything. I told you to see a partera." She put her arms around Amelia. "It will be fine, he will be fine. A strong boy, you will see." Her mother nodded, sure of herself, and Amelia wept on her shoulder.

***

"Your insurance has denied the sonogram. They say you have already reached your limit," the nurse said.

"Reached my limit?"

"You only get two and you've had both of them."

I started to shake. "But we're here because she's overdue and my doctor is trying to decide whether or not to induce today."

"I'm sorry, but we can't do it."

My tears turned to rage. "So you're saying my baby could die because of my insurance company?" I hugged my belly.

The woman shrugged and left.

I sat down in one of the hospital waiting room chairs, sobbing. My husband rubbed my back.

A woman in blue scrubs approached us. "Come with me," she said. "Hurry." We followed without question.

She led us into the sonogram room. "I heard the whole thing. This is bullshit." She motioned for me to lay on the table and she squirted gel onto the sonogram wand. "I'm doing this totally off the record. Just take the information back to your doctor and don't say anything to the hospital about this, ok?"

Of course," Greg said. I nodded and watched the screen. The images were eerie. We could see the details of her face, squished up inside me.

"The placenta is starting to calcify," she said. "Tell your doctor. The baby needs to come out today." She used a towel to wipe the gel off my body.

I got up off the table and hugged her. "Thank you," I said.

She smiled. "Good luck."

***

The partera gave her a cup of tea. It was hot, bitter.

"Tell me exactly what the doctor told you," she said in Spanish.

Amelia explained. She showed her the sonogram photos.

"I am so sorry, Amelia," the midwife said. "You will have to go to the hospital when it is time to give birth. This is beyond what I can do. There are some herbs I can give you that will make you go into labor early, if you want to get this over with, but I will be honest with you and say that they can be dangerous to your health too. Otherwise, you will have to wait until your body naturally goes into labor. It's your choice; I will support whichever you decide to do. I can also give you some herbs to calm your nerves and nourish your body."

Amelia sunk down into the overstuffed sofa and sipped her tea.

***

The fetal monitor screamed. "It's time to get your baby out." The midwife's tone betrayed the seriousness of the situation. With a final push, the baby slipped from my body. Her tiny voice screeched at the violence of birth. The doctor took her from the midwife to the neonatal exam table, gave her a large shot of Narcan to counteract the pain drugs I'd been given at the last minute. After a brief inspection, the doctor wrapped her in a blanket and lay her on my chest and I kissed her head and cried.

***

Amelia's mother helped her walk into the emergency room. Every few seconds Amelia bared down. Unable to fight the contractions, she groaned.

Two nurses ran to her. "Who is your doctor?" one of them asked. Amelia grimaced and pushed. "Dr Collier! We need you now!" one of them shouted.

A team of people scrambled around her. "Get her into a room!" one shouted. "Call labor and delivery, get someone down here! And pediatrics! We're having a baby people!" They carried her into an exam room.

"No," Amelia said. "Comprendo."

No one heard her in the whirlwind of activity. She was laying on a bed. How did she get here? Faces swirled around her. Someone moved her legs. She pushed. It hurt.

"The baby is crowning," a voice said. She looked around for her mother, but couldn't find her.

Someone placed a monitor on her stomach. Someone else put an oxygen mask on her face. She panicked.

"It's ok," a calm voice said. Someone stroked her hair. "Your baby is coming."

"No comprendo," Amelia whispered.

"I'm not getting a heartbeat."

Amelia beared down. She expelled the **fetus** into a riot of silence.

She caught a glimpse of his limp blue body as the doctors tried to resuscitate him. "Fetal death," one of them said. "Stillborn."

She saw the heartbreak in the nurse's eyes. "Would you like to hold him?" the nurse asked.

Amelia turned her head toward the silent monitors. Sin lágrimas, she told herself. Don't cry.

SARAH BROWN WEITZMAN

6. BEFORE ROE VS. WADE

Under a sky like curdled milk in a blue bowl
my childless friend of 40 years confesses to a 1958 abortion.

$100 to an elderly woman who laid her hips
on a rough, grayed towel, spread her knees apart

to stuff a narrow rubber hose cut from an enema bag
and stiffened with a copper strip up into her womb,

packed the cavity with wads of cotton, all tied together
by a string like a tampon. "Tomorrow pull the string

and *everything* will come out." Three bright drops of blood
on the towel, the color of induced labor hours later.

The wall of her womb pierced. Peritonitis. Hospital.
Penicillin. Police. But she was free of that unwanted child

or any child she could never have now. Her nipples oozed
droplets of sour milk staining her bras for weeks after.

© KONINKLIJKE BRILL NV, LEIDEN, 2020 | DOI:10.1163/9789004418820_006

ELIZABYTH A. HISCOX

7. THE DOUBLE HELIX IS NOT TWO-FACED, IT IS AN EMBRACE

My mother: the daughter of a Methodist minister, the daughter of a nuclear physicist.
Having wrestled with all the **entitlement** of eternity
And its instruction book, she had launched an internal **diversity** initiative with faith
And Watson and Crick[1] cuddling on the love seat of her soul.

My childhood was of her grand design: angels and angles were both important.
Hypotenuse and Gabriel sat on equal footing: bringing different, good news.

An entomologist who sang hymns as she pinned the insects, she had raised her voice
Heading off to college: defending her study of the frogs, the cadavers,
The **fetus**es, the butterflies and the **evidence-based** enlightened world
That such close attention can bring. Her father quoted a specific chapter and verse.

My childhood was Sundays of spirited services, and then science-
Based school projects (always **vulnerable** to her kind scrutiny). Gospels then gollywogs.

The minister was her step-father, the physicist her dead one.
And she had chosen love as a bonding agent long before I arrived. Two fathers, and a
Heavenly father and no worries. She was the first to explain biological sex, gender,
Transgender to me. The first to admit the limits of science in providing all we need.

© KONINKLIJKE BRILL NV, LEIDEN, 2020 | DOI:10.1163/9789004418820_007

In my childhood, *hypothesis* was one of the holiest words in our house—
It is a kind of leap of faith, an educated guess, and then the attempt to arrive
there.

NOTE

¹ Watson and Crick: Joint discoverers of the double helix structure of DNA.

SAMANTHA SCHAEFER

8. THAT LIGHT BILL

The pseudo-cento, *That light bill,* uses text from Gary Paulsen's *The Winter Room,* Anne Rice's *Servant of the Bone,* and *If Tomorrow Comes* by Sidney Sheldon.

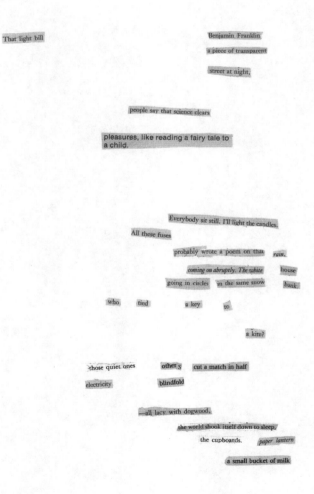

PART 2
#RESIST

It takes a village / to make a **fetus**.

LEE BEAVINGTON

9. KIDNAPPING CHILDREN AND CALVES
(OF A TENDER AGE)

When MSNBC reporter Rachel Maddow broke down in tears reporting on immigrant children being taken from their parents at the Mexico-U.S. border, she expressed the horror and grief felt by millions of viewers. She later tweeted an apology: "Ugh, I'm sorry. If nothing else, it is my job to actually be able to speak while I'm on TV." Yet her heartfelt response to the cruelty being perpetuated opened our hearts to empathy and anger and compassion. She showed her humanity in the face of the inhumane.

As I watched Maddow break her cool demeanor, dare to reveal her inner anguish, I welcomed my own tears. I cried for the children pulled from their parents, and I cried in disgust at a world that allows this to happen. When children, toddlers, and even babies are being stolen and put into 'tender age' shelters, I cry for their helplessness, and my own. Similarly helpless, in the nonhuman realm, fetal calves are harvested for the nutrient-rich serum extracted from their not-quite-formed hearts. I will return to fetal bovine serum later. For now, let's stick with the tender-aged humans.

Words to describe this traumatic experience of separating children from their families include "torture," "cruelty," "concentration camps," "held hostage," and "kidnapped." Each of these have been contested, yet when genocidal language is being used, when **diversity** is being denigrated, we are in dangerous terrain. As a parent and a human being, I can think of no greater torture than being forcibly separated from my young children. Tears are not to be apologized for in such cases, they are demanded.

These children are as young as one- or two-years-old. A friend recently shared a story on Facebook of a breastfeeding child being pulled from her mother by an immigration officer. Amidst all the comments of horror and disgust, mixed with compassion for this stolen child, one person replied, "Sad story. But I have to wonder why they are coming to the US in the first place." I refrain from social media debates. They are too often reactive, vitriolic, and rarely conducive to meaningful conversation. I prefer face-to-

© KONINKLIJKE BRILL NV, LEIDEN, 2020 | DOI:10.1163/9789004418820_009

face dialogue, or reading (and writing) well-thought out articles that provide detailed facts and thoughtful consideration to all points of view.

But I was triggered. Triggered by Rachel Maddow's **vulnerable** authenticity. Triggered by a one-year-old having to stand (crawl?) in court to represent themselves. Triggered by the stamping out of basic human rights. Triggered by the words "Sad story" in response to a child being taken from her mother.

I could no longer remain silent. My response was, "Of all the important questions that need to be asked right now, I don't believe this is one of them. Let's focus on the motives of those perpetuating cruelty, not those being subjected to it." The word *motive* comes from Latin, literally meaning something that *moves a person*. What can move a person to act from a place of such hate and harm? Part of this, I believe, stems from a lack of relationship to those being persecuted, and therefore a lack of compassion. When you don't understand the Other, you are much more willing to ignore or even cause suffering. How can I respond to children being tortured?

I turn to the practice of Bowing to our Adversaries. This is an exercise in gratitude and respect inspired by Buddhist teacher Thich Nhat Hanh. Caitriona Reed wrote these particular words to honor our adversaries:

Because the pain I feel when I witness the pain of the world is no less than your pain—you, who perpetuate destruction and cut yourselves off from the web of life—I bow to you in compassion and touch the Earth.

Because the pain of greed, alienation and fear is no less than the pain of sorrow for what is lost, I bow to you in compassion and touch the Earth.

For the power of my anger, arising from my passion for justice, I bow to you in gratitude and touch the Earth.

And so I thank this Facebook commenter whom I do not know, for allowing me to feel my sorrow, my anger, and my passion for justice more fully. Which has led me to writing these words.

The **entitlement** of those in power, those in places of great privilege, has inspired the Trump administration to oppose breastfeeding resolutions from the World Health Organization, to ban the **transgender**ed from serving in the military, to leave the Paris Climate Accord, and to put thousands of children into 'tender age' shelters. To resist these abuses of power, we must reflect, share and act.

***

Fortunately, *my* job does not require me to kidnap children. If it did, I'd be forced to quit. As science-fiction writer Robert A. Heinlein once said, "No intelligent man has any respect for an unjust law." But my job *does* require the use of animals of the nonhuman variety. For sixteen years, I have taught undergraduate biology labs at Kwantlen Polytechnic University.

When students walk into a science lab, they walk into a room full of assumptions. Here is a sterile place. A place where subjectivity is checked at the door. A place of experiment and dissection, justified in the name of science. A place where feeling, emotion, tears, and perhaps even ethics are to be repressed. Because there is a greater good at stake: the continued well-being of *Homo sapiens* through **evidence-based** science.

The work in this biology lab is assumed to be important, and is worth the ethical cost of whatever materials that need to be used. So when I hand students a vial of fetal bovine serum, I also hand them a hidden curriculum: this vial's contents supersede whatever went into its production. Their learning is more important than the harm being done to others.

Few would argue that science and mathematics are not pertinent to student education. Math is numbers, and science is purely objective, practiced with detached observation, so one may conclude, as Ben Spiecker wrote, that "we do not indoctrinate students in science." However, bias is unavoidable, and perceived objectivism can instill students with notions of anthropocentrism, discount non-scientific worldviews, and disregard the Other's perception or even wellbeing, whether that be fruit flies, lab rats, fetal calves, or humans. The assumption of human objectivity, the assumption of learning the truth, and the assumption of progress are also part of this "indoctrination." Recall Milgram's experiment where two-thirds of participants electro-shocked another person because they were objectively instructed to do so. "The extreme willingness of adults to go to almost any lengths on the command of an authority," wrote Milgram, suggests that authority figures, including lab instructors, can exercise extreme influence over their subjects. We follow authority. Are we hardwired for easy indoctrination? This might explain how Immigration and Customs Enforcement officers can pull distraught children from their parents.

For the power of my anger, arising from my passion for justice, I bow to you in gratitude and touch the Earth.

I have taught the advanced cell biology lab where my students frequently use cell culture, a technique that avoids experimenting on animals themselves because the cells can be grown in isolation and tested on directly. One lab called for fetal bovine serum (FBS), which is extracted from the hearts of

37

fetal calves in slaughterhouses. According to a study in *Alternatives to Lab Animals*, no anesthesia is used when FBS is drawn via cardiac puncture. In other words, a needle is inserted into the still pumping heart. (Brief aside: the title of the study I just referenced, "The use of fetal bovine serum: Ethical or scientific problem?," suggests that science and ethics are dichotomous. When did ethics stop being a problem of science?) This method of extracting FBS is justified due to the high demand for this fresh serum.

An animal welfare handout from Biowest, "The Serum Specialist," emphasizes that we should not "feel bad" about using fetal bovine serum. They contest that "There is no more of an ethical problem with 'killing bovine **fetus**es' than with 'killing adult animals.' They argue that mother cows are being killed anyway, so we might as well harvest the **fetus**. As a vegetarian with no interest in killing cattle of any age, this argument does not convince me to "feel bad" but rather to be morally outraged that these **fetus**es are referred to as "by-products." The Terrestrial Animal Health Code recommends that if there's any sign of consciousness of the **fetus**, to kill the **fetus** with a "blow to the head with a suitable blunt instrument."

For the power of my anger, arising from my passion for justice, I bow to you in gratitude and touch the Earth.

This was the first-time advanced cell biology was being taught at Kwantlen Polytechnic University, and everything was handled last minute. Thus I only realized the presence of FBS in the lab the day of its requisite usage. I opened the fridge and there sat the tray of fat blue-capped vials of a nondescript, undercooked pink liquid. I held one up close, at this fluid pulled from the heart of an animal no longer alive, and wondered what the hell I was going to do. I wondered too, about the journey this serum had taken: the mother cow in the slaughterhouse, the uterus sliced from her innards and slid down a "special stainless steel chute leading to the calf processing area," the worker who extracted this medium from the not-quite-a-calf's heart, the company that paid for its procurement ($600 per liter), the instructor who wrote its requirement for this lab, the lab technician who ordered it, and now the lab instructor who was about to give this to students. That's me.

There are moments in life where one has to decide what's more important: your duty or your integrity. This placed me in the "difficult deliberation" as Daniel Liston wrote, "of how much to give, when to offer a comment, and when to keep quiet." I ended up talking to my students in explicit detail about FBS, how it is obtained, and (partly in response to the shocked gasps from students) made the hopeful suggestion that perhaps one of them would, someday, develop a cost-effective synthetic alternative to FBS. I told them that one to two million bovine **fetus**es are harvested annually.

Then I gave them the vials. Is that the moment I became complicit?

I'm sure such a conversation is exceptionally unusual in a science lab; why, after all, would we spend time talking about ethics? There are cells to culture, experiments to run, critical dispositions to suppress, and **science-based** learning to be had. And although I perhaps played the role of honest heretic, it certainly did not feel like enough. I realize now, in the very writing of this piece, that as long as FBS is used in this lab I cannot be involved in its teaching. As Daniel Liston reminds us, we need to remember that "Teaching…is a **vulnerable** undertaking." To teach who we are, as Parker Palmer emphasizes, means being authentic to who we are.

When an authority figure gives you explicit and unequivocal directions, it can be difficult to voice disagreement. This can lead to indoctrination. As an educator—or even as a human being—remaining silent on a subject impresses a certain moral viewpoint. In education, is this not a form of indoctrination, when, as Spiecker explained, "The responses of these [learners] can only be: to accept and to believe"? What would be different if students had to obtain FBS themselves, and be engaged in the full story of its procurement? How many students would agree to extract FBS from a fetal calf's beating heart if I told them to do so?

Fetal bovine serum is commonly used in cell culture for vaccine production, cloning, *in vitro* fertilization and biotechnology research. The human benefit is irrefutable. However, it should be noted that since FBS is not a defined medium, its constituent components vary depending on the fetal calf used as a source. This introduces uncontrolled variables into cell culture experiments, something science abhors.

Some have argued that the **fetus**es do not feel pain, yet the scientific evidence suggests otherwise. At the very least, we cannot know for certain at what stage in development fetal calves do, or do not, feel pain. Is our benefit worth the ethical cost of emptying these hearts? Certainly, the complete lack of relationship between FBS and its source contributes to its unabated usage.

Without relationship, there is less capacity for empathy. Remember Rachel Maddow's on-air tears: she inspires our path toward compassion. And so I cry for each child kidnapped from their parents. I cry for each fetal calf whose heart is sucked dry every 20 seconds of every day to fulfill our scientific duty. I cry for the fetal calf whose heart I gave away to my students. I offer this poem to share her story, in the hope that these words might move you, my dear readers.

For the power of my anger, arising from my passion for justice, I bow to you in gratitude and touch the Earth.

NEW LIFE OR FBS

I.
The fridge is full of blood—
baby cow blood—
in plastic vials, frozen
row upon row of bright blue caps

I pull out the tray—
how many calves did it take?

Fetal bovine serum—
a nutrient soup
so rich with life
we kill to get at it.

My students wait for their fill

No lab rats in this lab
our culture is cellular—
we divide cells
pick everything apart
until it ceases to work

A heartless broth—

  albumin bilirubin
   hemoglobin insulin
    growth hormone glucose
     calcium cortisol cholesterol
      thyroxine testosterone parathormone
        protein prolactin phosphate potassium progesterone
         follicle-stimulating hormone

bits of baby cow

A perfect mix for new life—
for cancer's sake

The calf was born to die.
To sit in a vial
that now thaws in my hand.
FBS is what is left of you
the lab manual censors your story

II.
Dear Calf,

It begins with your mother
slaughtered too soon.
You are born an orphan
but only briefly

You are cut from the womb—
an emergency cesarean.
A **fetus** that has no time
to conceive her mother's death.

They are after your heart—

You slide down a metal chute
take your first gasp of air.
Your heart still beating
is cut out

processed like an artichoke

Serum is extracted
with no anesthetic or ethic—
you are still gasping for air
a syringe empties your heart

III.
I pass a vial to each student
we hold your fetal life in our hands

hands that have shed no blood.

We are scientists after all

Ready

to save a life by taking a life.

This science is above story
above sentiment

The silence of every calf
quietly buried in our hearts

I speak
but I am too late

SHALEN LOWELL

10. WHAT DOES TRANSGENDER LOOK LIKE?

I.
Discard all shades of plaid
those Vans
the undercut
the wacky hair and quirky personality.

(Social suicide, cultural normativity,
media-enforced heterocisnormativity)

In the fetal position
hiding your depression from friends, family, work
for months
and months
and months
and months on end—

painting your own fake face
(you don't *look* like you have depression)
long days, longer nights, longer
feelings of misplacement and anatomical dysphoria

you barely understand yourself.

The acronym reads lgBTQia
but you couldn't feel more alone,
less represented—
a **transgender**/genderfluid bisexual/questioning pansexual/invisible
polysexual—
where "home" reads as "alone," "claustrophobia," and "trigger."

© KONINKLIJKE BRILL NV, LEIDEN, 2020 | DOI:10.1163/9789004418820_010

II.
The pound sign:
My heart pounding
when I hear the words—
"I am **transgender**"—
escape from one breath.

The hashtag:
call me whatever gender you like,
just never "*lady.*"

My day is a poem of politically charged hashtags:
#GenderConfusion
#TransPeopleAreValid

My life a series of "coming outs."

#GenderfluidIsAValidTransIdentity
(Am I banned from saying that, too?)

MINADORA MACHERET

11. WOMAN WITH PCOS LINGERS ON THE POSSIBILITIES OF SCIENCE

At 13 I was promised
that birth control would save
my body from self-harm. That those hormones help
blind the senses, forget about disease
as it rots away your DNA.
But my body still aches,
the BC never helped
just poisoned my mind
& made me believe
I could jump off buildings.

My father tells everyone I'm his strongest child,
as a doctor states my disease is only temporary.
16 years is only temporary as a canary
plunging into caverns, using joy to predict death.
My canary is my heart's palpitations
a harmless hiccup I am to monitor
because women do not feel pain
as men do during a heart attack.

Research isn't looking for **evidence-based** cures
or ways to lessen female pain.
Scientists are interested in afflictions
that all humans possess at least once
in a life time. As you call to confirm
that I will house-sit for you
and tell me *I'm a life-saver*.

You told me not to worry
about the Clematis blooming

© KONINKLIJKE BRILL NV, LEIDEN, 2020 | DOI:10.1163/9789004418820_011

wavy purple petals creeping higher
than the porch light.
Five years had passed without any growth,
only temporary you repeated
as you showed me the house
and the ways to care for it.

You told me the mouse infestation
was only temporary. I believed the poison
would kill them. The way your lungs collapsed
from scar tissue build-up
and you huddled on your couch
a breathing machine whirring
forcing oxygen, an act of temporality.

You left me your home for five months
and I watched the Clematis blossom, wrapping its vines
excitedly on the post you had placed
to nurture the plant's curiosity.

Sometimes you trick the system
to breathe without an oxygen machine.
To prompt the brain to cradle new lungs. No longer full of scar
tissue. This is only temporary
the doctors warn.

And I wonder how DNA sequences recall
the body before damage. How you must wrap your brain
with a veil. To trick the body to continue living.

Much like the doctors the night
of your double-lung transplant. As the cavity
of the ceiling split open to let the rain in.

KAREN L. FRANK

12. HALF A SCHROEDINGER

My mind is not wandering in a mist
of thought experiments and conjecture
when I say I and all my photons
are entangled with multivarious I's
and all their photons.
So out there, in other landscapes, live
other women within locked containers,
neither alive nor dead
vulnerable because no one registers our heartbeats,
grounding our sense of self in our locality—
the insides of secured chambers—
reclining in superpositioned perplexity,
protected from change but
poised for our coins to flip.
Should I awaken to my own complexity
and strike out of the cage on my own
then this infinitude of diverse females
will also awake, alive or dead.
All second shoes will hit the floor
and the kitties will be out of the box,
free to be one with the universe.

KRIS HARRINGTON

13. BUBBLES

The bubbles floated into the gymnasium at St. Paul's, one, two, three, and then more than I could count, drifting over the tables where supplies were sorted into categories. Signs in both English and Spanish gave instructions for how items were to be rationed. Milk, eggs, and flour, one per family. One bottle of shampoo. Two canned goods. One box of cereal. I saw the bubbles before I saw the children, so many of them, so tiny, shorter in height than my waist. It was 95 degrees at 10:00 a.m. on a Saturday, and even though the distribution wasn't set to begin until 11:00, the families lined up early for food and necessities.

The ICE raid at Fresh Mark in Salem, Ohio on June 20, 2018 was the largest domestic workplace ICE raid in more than ten years, and 146 migrant workers were arrested, loaded on buses, and taken to prisons. A migrant worker, documented or not, is an easy target during these days of the ramped-up xenophobia, ushered in by the build-that-wall Trump presidency. A local man who boasted his support for both Trump and the philosophy of the wall openly took credit for the call that resulted in the ICE raid. After a year-long investigation, agents descended upon the meat packing plant with guns, buses, armed trucks, and a helicopter. I drove past that meat-packing plant every day on the way to and from my university lecturer job, where I teach the works of great thinkers like Plato, Woolf, King, and Mead to first-year college students. When I heard of the Fresh Mark raid, I was shocked and then ashamed to learn how little I knew of the community.

The quickest position for me to take as a resister is one of anger at the man (yes, a White man) who notified the authorities, at Trump, at the GOP, at the neighbors I don't count among the good and righteous. I have a button and a bumper sticker with the word RESIST in white on a black background. I call and write my representatives, donate to the ACLU, sign petitions, push voter registration. I wore a pink hat and marched in Washington D.C. And like so many of my peers, I mostly direct my energy outward into saying what I have to say, into raising awareness through words and demonstrations, into speaking up for the **vulnerable** among us.

But the real work of resistance I learned that day at St. Paul's, is the resistance I faced within myself. I was compelled to investigate my dual motives. Why do I resist? Is resistance a true commitment or is it how I define me to me? Is it both?

Most of the migrant workers at Fresh Mark were from Guatemala, and they had sought asylum in the United States after fleeing civil wars and gang violence in their homeland. At the meat-packing plant, they worked for substandard wages to support their families, to keep their children safe from rape and torture. I'd read stories about young men barely surviving the forced and bloody MS-13 initiation, only to be murdered later for some perceived transgression or for trying to get out, their disemboweled bodies strung from bridges. I'd read stories of young women and girls who disappeared into the dark world of sex slavery. The migrants had fled these fears years before, settled, found homes and jobs in Ohio.

Yanked from the meat-packing line, they now waited in cells, for deportation, release, or further detainment. Their families no longer had an income. The plan to distribute food and basic supplies came together quickly among community leaders and the sisters at St. Paul's. I found myself pulled along. I wish I could say that there was a moment when I boldly decided to engage, but that wasn't the case. I tip-toed into action. I was asked by a friend to collect items, and so my dining room table became piled with boxes of diapers, packages of maxi-pads, and giant bear-shaped tubs of animal crackers, which seemed oddly innocent in context. On the morning of June 30, ten days after the raid, my husband, our daughters, and I traveled to St. Paul's with a car full of supplies and heads full of the desire to do something more than we'd done before. Ideal motives, for sure, on a day that turned out to be one that required the direct and practical more than the intellectual.

One of the other volunteers had purchased bottles of bubbles to occupy the children while they waited in line. And seeing those bubbles floating through the gymnasium transformed the abstract idea of those families into reality for me. I turned from my work of making ham sandwiches for brown bag lunches and took in the scene. Children were piled on mothers' laps or standing in small clusters while they waited their turns. None of the people I saw fit the urchin image that is fed to us through the pictures on our screens. The children's clothes were clean and unwrinkled, their hair combed and neatly styled, and they were bright-eyed and excited. A little boy wearing a Chicago Bulls cap was slung with fabric to his mothers' back, and he peeked curiously over her shoulder. The line of people stretched out into parking lot, into the heat-thick Ohio midday, where women held umbrellas over their children's heads to protect them from the sun. I found out later that we passed out 150 lunches, exhausting our supply, and that we saw 72 families.

Sister Rene told us about the police cruisers across the street. She'd already sent the press cameras away. She seemed too calm as she passed on this information, and the gravity of what I didn't know struck me hard. Someone else would handle the press and the police. Someone else would know the exact rights, the exact words. As a teacher and a mother, I was used to being in charge or at least at the top of the chain. My skills that day were limited. I felt bloated with privilege. Until that point, I realized, I hadn't been resisting as much as I'd been staying safely on the fringes of resistance.

The volunteers were grouped into those who could speak Spanish and those who couldn't. The first group would guide the Guatemalan families through the tables of supplies, assisting in selection. Those of us volunteers who couldn't speak Spanish were assigned to various jobs. I became sharply aware of how utterly unprepared I was. For years, I had counted myself as one of the smart ones, but now I felt dumb and tongue tied with my Sesame Street Spanish and my good intentions. I told myself that I deserved it, this rupturing of my naiveté. I moved self-consciously from one task to the next, refilling the milk and egg table, passing out lunches, loading cars, distributing bottles of warm water. One of the other helpers told me that she'd stashed some water in the refrigerator for the volunteers "so that it'll be nice and cold for us." I wouldn't allow myself to drink the cold water as a kind of penance. I would drink warm water, too—a weird attempt to equalize what was glaringly unequal.

I expected to feel good about my work that day. I expected to feel the same boost that I felt when I marched or rallied. Instead, I felt selfish and spoiled as I carried bottled water through the growing crowd, minding my elbows, awkwardly asking "aqua?" and passing out bottles two and three at a time. One small giggling girl and her two sisters, all dressed in bright blue were puffing through their bubble wands as hard as they could, their tiny hands slick with soap, their eyes full of delight. Their laughter took me by surprise. I looked toward the girls' mother, and our eyes connected. I noticed the sling around her shoulder, a tiny bump in the fabric at her hip. A baby. Four babies.

I started think about how an event can split a life into a before and an after, slice it wide open. I wondered how much these girls would remember. I wondered if they'd get an after. But their giggles also grounded me and reminded me that people want to laugh, that joy is our default, and that we humans complicate our lives so much that we squint to find joy most days, if we find it at all. We want to love. We are born for it—the little ones among us still know—but so much else gets in the way. Else is a big word. It fills up our lives where the love should be.

Plato's escaped prisoner emerged from the shadows to see reflections of objects, then the objects themselves, then the greater light of the philosopher, and when he returned to the cave, he was ridiculed. It is basic to our nature to avoid the vulnerability of being the other, and so we sometimes hesitate and hedge more than we should. The spiritual leaders of generations have all tried to communicate this truth to us, but the notion that we must face ourselves gets lost in the pulled quotes. Margaret Mead's most famous words are "Never doubt that a small group of thoughtful, committed citizens can change the world; indeed, it's the only thing that ever has." But Mead also told us that we need to tear it all down first. We can't grasp onto parts out of fear and expect real difference.

Resistance requires equal parts of fear, trust, and love. What we love, we can lose. We try to prevent one way of losing only to open another way. In trying not to lose their children to the violence of their day-to-day lives, these families made themselves **vulnerable** to the fickle and brutish American system. Maybe we're all unsafe right now, and it sure seems that way. In trying not to lose our jobs, our relationships, our peace of mind, we limit how we make ourselves **vulnerable**. Being **vulnerable** is frightening, and when we have the privilege of not choosing it, it's easy for us to be too busy.

I meekly accept that my purpose in this resistance is not merely to hand wring and to make a few signs. My job is to collect, and my job is to show up, and, yes, to learn a little Spanish because these families will need more from me in the days until they are together again, if those reunions happen at all. I want to believe in their after, though, and maybe that's a kind of vulnerability, too.

That morning at St. Paul's, I wished I knew their word for bubbles so that I might share that fleeting joyful moment with the little girls, stair steps in height and dressed alike to be easily spotted in a crowd, like my own daughters when they were that small. They giggled and puffed, and I stepped aside, giving the bubbles a clear path, letting them float for as long as they would, up into the sky above all our heads.

FRANKLIN K. R. CLINE

14. THE EASE AND DIFFICULTY OF HATING AND LOVING ONE'S SELF

a fly bonks itself against
a screen, seeing the trees

not able to get to them
generally not getting it

feeling morose today and divided
the mixedblood sleeps

alone on a twin mattress
I can't find Santee's book, too bad

I've been thinking about it
I've been driving around

without my driver's license
got refused service for trying to use

my tribal ID at a bar
dust is thickening on the tops of things

there's some scene in some movie where some character
says *I have so much to give* pleadingly

but I can't remember the context
as far as I can tell the fly is going to do one of three things

die in my apartment, propagate
in my apartment, or leave my apartment

© KONINKLIJKE BRILL NV, LEIDEN, 2020 | DOI:10.1163/9789004418820_014

and either die or propagate
the mixedblood is feeling morose today and wishing I had some

gin or something maybe some pills
maybe instead of morose I mean **vulnerable**

not sure what the difference is or
if they inform each other

if they talk to each other the way the fly
talks to the screen as it yearns to talk to the trees

BEN PAULUS

15. SEVEN THOUGHTS ABOUT BUTTERFLIES

I think of **vulnerable**
butterflies, their wet wings their **entitlement**
to flight, but not flight. The **diversity**
of deaths that await them as they **transgender**
from caterpillar to fly-by, from **fetus**
to angel, despite all the **evidence**. **Based**

on a hunch, **transgender**
from sexless to sexed, mate in mid-air based
on luck and (after the wings dry) the **fetus-**
shaped patterns painted there. **Diversity**
of shape and shade, butterfly **entitlement**
to sex the swap for being **vulnerable**

prey. The sheer **diversity**
of horrors that awaits. They're **vulnerable**
to windshields, and car grills, our **entitlement**
to speed down gravel roads—sixty-five our **fetus**
birthright, proven in court, a true **science-based**
fact. Like caterpillars—their trans-**transgender**

reality: a **fetus**
that walks, not female—not male—as **transgender**
as transgender does. Voracious eating-based
life, pre-sex! Imagine such **entitlement**!
to live pre-gender: to be **vulnerable**
not to lust—only to the **diversity**

of hungers. **Entitlement**
is the wisdom of wasps: the **diversity**
of tools they use to plant eggs in **vulnerable**

caterpillar flesh: ovipositor-based
tortures; maggot death. And wasps, too, **transgender**:
shift sex as needed by the hive; each **fetus**

gender (worker, drone, mate) is determined based
on alien algorithms, each **fetus**
matched to mission, to role, to task, **transgender**
by intent. And that system **vulnerable**
to invasion by a **diversity**
of parasites. The jungle's **entitlement**

   to eat the **vulnerable** is based
   on the **entitlement** of every **fetus**
   to choose **diversity**, to choose **transgender**.

MICHELLE BONCZEK EVORY

16. IT TAKES A VILLAGE

to make a **fetus**. And nurses
dressed in light green allheart scrubs
to demonstrate on their own bodies
where to insert the needle, the barely noticed
angle of metal, between bellybutton
and pelvis, a different inch each night.
Because you will need ultrasounds, blood tests,
acupuncture, massages, vitamins, and prayers.
Because you will tire of explaining FSG, HSG,
IUI, ICSI, PCT, SET, and unexplained infertility
to family members and friends—many women
themselves, splinters of their children's DNA
orbiting their brains like moons. Fathers
who would prefer to just hear you say *I'm expecting*
instead of **science-based** *evidence &* **evidence-based**
decisions. But what you can expect is the many times
you will describe the steps of IVF to your younger
sister—estradiol after ovulation to prepare
the body, Lupron to suppress ovulation once
you bleed, Follistim to stimulate egg growth, Ovidrel
to release the egg. And then, that dream of a vortex
of embryos floating like sunlit dust, the drive
to the clinic, anesthesia, egg retrieval, and recovery
while strangers in masks, eyes doming microscopes,
insert his sperm into your egg, and see.

© KONINKLIJKE BRILL NV, LEIDEN, 2020 | DOI:10.1163/9789004418820_016

SCOTT M. BADE

17. THE CAPITAL OF FAILURE

I fail each morning bright with tumescence's essence
draining night's great feats. So much blood and only
the bathroom willing to accept the dream is over, has been
since first snooze, second elbow. When house finch flies
away after nest is plundered, eggs a muddle beneath lamp-
post, is that an understanding of failure? I remember sobs
sabotaging her speech as she exited the bathroom,
mystery of miscarriage muddling that spring. Surely
there is more than one ailment bound up in failure.
What ails me is that which sustains, some of the time,
and most of the pain. Funny how the rhyme inflates it,
just as self-inflicted muscular tearing via strenuous
lifting leads to pecs like pillows and admiring minutes
in front of mirrors. When I play my guitar, failure sings
its greatest hits. Admitting failure does not constitute
maturity. It capitalizes it, thus creating a strangely
compelling desire for larger and greater ways to fail.
For example, see nearly all of what's on television and
the current president of the United States. There is fire
in failure, a lure, something to rue when the real is all
that's left to leaf through, to feel. And the hook knows
failure of fish sight. And feet know the failure of shoes.
Not walking pain but the knowledge terrain speaks through
your soles. Failing open and failing closed make our
world navigable but not infallible. Without failure only
bland success. Boredom is a failure of imagination. 9/11
is a failure of a nation. Almost has been writing it, nearly
perfectly, since the 12th century. Like some dreams, failure
is both light and heavy. I mean creams, too. Light behaves
as wave and particle. So too failure when memed
and snapped. A winner said failure is a huge part

© KONINKLIJKE BRILL NV, LEIDEN, 2020 | DOI:10.1163/9789004418820_017

of winning. They pointed to Donald Trump as an **evidence-based** example of the capital of failure, which points back to this poem and its many failures. Many Larry Levis poems are rooms full of the *fatigued aftertaste of failure*. A failing valve in my heart hums a song, its rhythm captivating, like a blues. So much failure isn't here, which puts it here. Often, I've found myself standing alone at the window imagining how one squirrel lost part of its tail. Fighting, I imagine. But for what? A mate? What's right? But then losing. Defeat a feat conquered and turned to fuel or, if nothing else, a talisman and chant, when everything's messed, tail-less body holding a tale's body, this piece, the bricks and lies of it, tangible and real, every morning on the lawn in front of a bleached house, in mirror of your mirror: fail, your fail, your fail, your failyourfailyourfailyour

PART 3

EVIDENCE

Transgendered others stuck in the cracks,
I would need to trust my colleague in science;
Another **evidence-based** day.

18. FIELD NOTES & MARGINALIA

One of my university colleagues, a molecular biologist, had arranged to meet me in DC for a tour of the natural history museum where my husband, an organismal biologist, works. With him were his wife and two teenaged children. As we walked to the metro after the tour, passing the Old Post Office, the former home of the National Endowment of the Humanities where I once reviewed proposals, I heard his son's voice, but not the words. To my "what did he say?" his father responded, "an abortion truck, or, rather, anti-abortion truck." Though I didn't want to look, my eye nevertheless caught the blurry red of what I assumed was a **fetus**.

We had begun the day by catching an exhibit of science illustrations at the American Association for the Advancement of Science. Though there was no discernible organizational strategy to the presentation of illustrations, all reflected **diversity**, the **diversity** of the world in which we live and a diversity of artistic responses to the question I found myself asking: "What is science?" The image on the truck used assumptions about scientific representation for rhetorical purpose.

But my question was not about rhetoric. The exhibit hung surprisingly whimsical representations of nature beside others with more clearly pedagogical aims, from "The

Bryan Shawn Wang July 24, 2018
A visitor to the city, I'd lost all sense of direction, but scanning the map later, I saw that we were walking north on 12th Street NW from the museum. The EPA headquarters was on our left; the Old Post Office, now home to the Trump International Hotel, on our right.

Bryan Shawn Wang July 24, 2018
Every afternoon for several weeks last fall, my children and their classmates were met at school dismissal by pro-life advocates displaying large images of fetuses and distributing pamphlets about abortion, pedophilia, and rape. Perhaps this had inured my son and daughter to such tactics; they didn't give the truck a second glance.

Bryan Shawn Wang July 24, 2018
Thinking on the nature of diversity has me envisioning a branching tree, with unifying connections and with a fractal quality.

Bryan Shawn Wang July 24, 2018
Your question gave me pause. Later in the essay, you note how the approach of Aristotle *et al.* to "*science/ scientia*" involved description (and, by implication, close observation) and communication. That seems apt here, too. Are description and communication the primary intents of scientific illustration? Can we judge an illustration "scientific" as long as it seeks to accomplish these aims?

Mysterious Oarfish" rendered in comic book frames, to a wonderful lesson on how to draw a Zoea, and onto a step-by-step illustration of how a tidal mill pond works. There were three-dimensional works of leafy landscapes and arboreal creatures with no apparent concern for scale; and there were interpretations of atoms as well as of cancer cells attacking sugar.

My colleague gave his camera to his daughter to take pictures. He was not just keeping her busy but, I assumed, using her as our teachers' aide to collect images we might use.

Two years earlier, I had approached this biology colleague at a faculty meeting. We had only spoken to one another once before, and I had no idea what he even looked like. I asked another colleague to identify him at the faculty meeting, so I could thank him in person for a letter of recommendation he had written a student for a highly competitive scholarship. In science. Before that, we had talked on the phone about that letter. I had heard, too, from my colleagues in English, that he had participated in a workshop on writing across the disciplines. That was a good sign. Lastly, I had noticed in the college's research magazine that he had published a short story and a poem. I did not know he had a Ph.D. from MIT, that he had been in industry, or that, according to one of his colleagues, "I had nabbed the most brilliant" scientist on the faculty, a spontaneous response to learning he and I were developing a course we planned to co-teach. If I had known any of those things, I might not have approached him about an

> **Bryan Shawn Wang** July 24, 2018
> For the record: I believe the picture intended to illustrate the structure of sugar molecules that decorate the surface of cancer cells, although in truth, the forms in the graphic might just as easily have represented alien figures doing battle.

> **Bryan Shawn Wang** July 24, 2018
> In that phone call, I found a colleague who could be at once blunt, caring, and persuasive. You suggested I back up my assertions with more evidence and employ specificity over generalities. You didn't point out that, as a scientist, I should have known better.

> **Bryan Shawn Wang** July 24, 2028
> My colleagues in science occasionally surrender to exaggeration.

> **Bryan Shawn Wang** July 24, 2018
> As I remember the faculty meeting, we approached one another. I suspect we were equally intrigued and equally intimidated.

idea I had for an interdisciplinary biology and humanities course.

Or maybe I would have.

More than twenty years earlier, when I taught at a college in Kansas that was also revamping its general education requirements, one of my colleagues in chemistry mentioned a course the chair of the new program, an English professor, had suggested he offer: The Periodic Table. Even though I knew the likely source for the suggestion, Primo Levi's book of the same name, I guffawed. He said, "So, what would you do?" And I said, "That's easy, From Alchemy to Chemistry." Did I mention that my area of study is medieval and early modern literature? That is to say, not an auspicious field of study for a "**science-based**" or "**evidence-based**" course, especially if you have a narrow understanding of "science" or "evidence." You might not be surprised by my response to the chemist who told me we would be teaching it together in the fall: "Are you crazy?"

I had integrated science into my literature courses with a lab examination of a cadaver, preceded by a walk in a cemetery, to complement Frankenstein and an introduction to bats through museum specimens and a trek to a cave filled with them for Dracula, both experiences provided by science faculty, chemists and biologists. Still, the thought of teaching an entire semester with someone in science was daunting. I had, and have, a very good sense of what I don't know, and a fear of what I might not be able to learn under pressure of time or at all.

> **Bryan Shawn Wang** July 24, 2018
> I'd wager that many students wouldn't mind some literature in their science courses, too.

> **Bryan Shawn Wang** July 24, 2018
> Nor would they mind field trips like these!

To accept the challenge, I would need to trust my colleague in science: that he wouldn't think I was stupid, or ignorant, or slow, or obtuse. I knew it was probably a good thing for students to see their teachers as **vulnerable** yet willing to fail and to work with someone whose academic orientation was so radically different, that the educational endeavor really is about learning, and not just for students.

Therefore, our course, Alchemy to Chemistry, integrating science and the humanities, did not "oppose" our two cultures, as C.P. Snow's article might have anticipated or feared. It juxtaposed methodologies, text-based literary interpretation with weekly labs replicating or demonstrating experiments, from pre-Christian Greek fire to Newton's tests on acid and into the twentieth century with Marie Curie.

More than twenty years later, at another college, I thought I had finally found a scientist on the faculty who might be willing to engage in a dialogue between science and literature, someone interested in having conversations that could extend beyond one specific research specialty to consider how we got there. It was a hunch, something easier to credit, perhaps, from someone who teaches medieval romance with its supernatural occurrences than for someone who looks at cells through a microscope. Never mind that molecular biology was not exactly ingrained as a discipline when I went to a small liberal arts college at the start of the 1970's. Maybe there had been a course devoted to the subject; I don't

Bryan Shawn Wang July 24, 2018
Another kind of trust: while I understand there's much to be learned from observing another's vulnerabilities and failures, and that teaching certainly requires humility, I also believe students need sages and guides with authority. Thank goodness you have that authority (and experience and knowledge) in "your half" of our course.

Bryan Shawn Wang July 24, 2018
Whether scientist, humanist, or artist, I think we all work from hunches. And, what's more, although the hunch provides a starting point, we're willing, even compelled, to examine it, assess it, and refine or redirect or relegate it to the trash bin in the face of contrary evidence.

Bryan Shawn Wang July 24, 2018
There was little room in my undergraduate science curriculum for even a passing mention of the ideas, events, and figures that contributed to pre-20th century scientific advances. There was even less room for art.

recall, probably because I would never have enrolled in it.

While "molecular biology" had been developing as a field and, therefore, was familiar as a word combination, having been coined in the nineteenth century, certain other terms were not: according to the sacred text of English majors, the *Oxford English Dictionary*, "**evidence-based**" would initially appear after I began teaching in the early 1980's and the word "**trans-gender**" not until the year I graduated college. The words never came up in the documents I proofread for an insurance company in Los Angeles before I left for graduate school.

The word "**science-based**" was used rather differently than it is now, though it originally appeared in a university publication. Indeed, the three appearances of the adjectival phrase provide a lesson in how words and concepts change with the times, both culturally and politically. The first quotation, from the *Dublin University Magazine* in 1850, refers to "a thoroughly **science-based** knowledge of the principles of beauty" that is "not a mere dilettante smattering of pictures, statues, or buildings." The second is from *The Economist* (1962), quoting Lord Hailsham's claim that "An Industry can be **science-based**,...and yet do little or no actual research." Those two quotations suggest a wrestling with what can be **science-based**, what entitles use of the term. The last example, occurring nearly 50 years later, introduces the more common associations with the modifier: "We have excellent predictive tools in the form of **science-based** models" (OED).

Bryan Shawn Wang July 24, 2018
To most, the idea of crossing gender boundaries was (and is) likely even more baffling than the thought of crossing disciplinary borders.

Bryan Shawn Wang July 24, 2018
Tangentially, perhaps one potential danger of interdisciplinary work is taking, or being perceived as taking, a dilettante's approach to the "other" discipline. How do interdisciplinary folk give two (or more) fields thorough (not necessarily science-based) treatment when those who remain in one discipline devote their entire working lives to just one? Again, I'm grateful to be *sharing* my journey into integration with you.

Despite a college education that skipped any study of the predictive tools that have come to define "**science-based** models"—math and computers—I was aware of the need to read the disciplines in relation to one another, going so far as to propose an honors program that did just that. (I was poo-poohed with the usual, everyone here is an honors student, though then, as now, my ideal of an honors program had nothing to do with entitlement, the perceived, or presumptively assessed, smartness of students but with creative approaches to curricula that I realized even then would be resisted).

> **Bryan Shawn Wang** July 24, 2018
> Something else the disciplines have in common: the need to "read" (and listen to) other's work in a way that's intentional, critical, generous, and unhurried.

Ideas and ideals are one thing, reality another. I had last taken a chemistry course in high school. My college biology course was ornithology; we looked at birds through binoculars, not at their feathers or tissues through microscopes. Reading the *New York Times Science* section on Tuesdays or random *Science* magazines was no substitute for a systematic study of organic chemistry, the area of my first co-teacher, or molecular biology, the area of my impending second one.

> **Bryan Shawn Wang** July 24, 2018
> Absent growth, or change, one's own sphere—bubble—can be a rather comfortable place.

What makes someone willing to venture into unknown, perhaps unfriendly, certainly terrifying territory?

> **Bryan Shawn Wang** July 24, 2018
> Foolhardiness? Or faith? Wanderlust?

As a graduate student, I was aware of the way English faculty responded to the perceived threat from the sciences, what seemed then assumptions about the reward-value for scientific research that cast doubt on the validity of humanities research, at least when salaries were published. The culture wars further impacted the discussion, no doubt, but my perception of the effect of the sciences on English was limited to noticing ever-increasing expectations when it came to the number of publications required for tenure and promotion. I can't recall any expressed animus between science and English departments; the two units seemed remote from one another. My positions at small colleges, on the other hand, belied the war: the boundaries are less clear when everyone knows everyone. Indeed, at one college, those of us who did research, and most did not, exchanged papers, never mind how disparate our fields—a chemist and biologist read my papers, and I read theirs. Getting to know chemists and biologists began to influence both my creative and academic writing: I wrote poems on scientific methods—trapping, measuring, drawing; and I suddenly noticed chemistry in Milton's *Paradise Lost* and Stoker's *Dracula*, observations that would later be developed into scholarly articles. I would even write an article on animals in one of Chaucer's *Canterbury Tales* with a biologist, the one with whom I had exchanged scholarly articles years earlier.

The political climate has impacted what gets written and by whom, and, therefore, what gets taught and to whom, since well before I was a graduate student. In the Middle Ages, priests studied readings of the Bible, the Desert Fathers, and commentaries at Oxford; in Victorian London, working class men were encouraged to read literature and philosophy; and in the present, American students learn how to write by focusing on timely themes such as ethics or community service or climate change or identity, etc. The diminishing interest in the humanities,

Bryan Shawn Wang July 24, 2018
If publications are the coin of the academic realm, what's the proper exchange rate among the fields? But maybe this is the very kind of question that promotes hostility between the disciplines. Other, less divisive questions: what's the balance between quality and quantity when it comes to publications? how to judge quality? and why the inflationary pressure on quantity, anyway?

Bryan Shawn Wang July 24, 2018
You're talking about engaging colleagues in a deeply productive way, not simply recognizing faces on campus. For one to know another requires commitment and time and a willingness to expose ourselves and, yeah, our vulnerabilities.

and the concomitant rise of majors in business, computer science and the sciences, can also be ascribed to a political climate that privileges the practical or denigrates what is perceived to be impractical or dangerous with its attention to ideas that while "**evidence-based**," as understood in rhetoric, is certainly not "**science-based**," as understood in the common parlance.

> **Bryan Shawn Wang** July 24, 2018
> An environment that conflates opinions (or lies) with facts / evidence denigrates education and scholarship in all fields.

And that takes me back to the question I found myself asking at the AAAS exhibit of science illustrators. A lovely, detailed picture of a flower was reminiscent of a seventeenth-century representation of a flower by Maria Sibylla Merian. In 1699, was it a scientific illustration?

> **Bryan Shawn Wang** July 24, 2018
> How about today?

That is the question that informs the course my colleague in molecular biology and I will confront in our course From Beast Books to Resurrecting Dinosaurs. The early literature the course covers concerns *scientia*, the Latin root of science that means knowledge: Aristotle, Pliny, Albertus Magnus, bestiaries, different ways knowledge seekers sought to understand the world. Albertus claimed to have described what he saw; he talked to people about what they saw. When the biologist with whom I developed the course suggested the second part of its title, I asked if that wasn't a little much, though I expressed appreciation for the connection I assumed he was making to the allegorical representations of animals in the Middle Ages. His response was a correction: that's what those in the field call it. That fact is still extraordinary to me for creating an unexpected continuity between early *scientia* and science. I am interested in what happens to words as they move through the

> **Bryan Shawn Wang** July 24, 2018
> Later in the course, we'll talk about how scientists sought to explain these observations, how they gathered evidence in favor of some possible explanations and against others, and how modern efforts to engineer nature stem from and continue to test our mechanistic understanding of biology. From *scientia* to science.

centuries into the now. The methodological shifts are also compelling, the way they parallel developing technologies—whether of paper or the printing press, an electronic screen or the internet, lenses that corrected vision or later more powerful lenses that magnify cells, and on and on.

Working with those in science is like developing a new lens, creating a new medium. Sometimes I am provoked to question what the lens reveals: how to make sense of the microscopic, of a process that can snip the seemingly invisible to create something that didn't exist before. Editing. It's what molecular biologists and poets do.

I have been promised something that glows. We'll talk about it in our different languages, and we'll make connections among them, preparing the next generation to participate in the conversation, one that began a very long time ago, and one that our students will become responsible for extending deep into the future. Resistance is believing such things are possible, teaching as if they are, and then committing the attempt to words, like this, right here.

Bryan Shawn Wang July 24, 2018
The AAAS exhibit of scientific illustrations referred to the "unseen" as the microscopic, the cosmic, the extinct—but the term could also apply to the supernatural.

Bryan Shawn Wang July 24, 2018
Students in the course will transfer a gene from a luminescent jellyfish into bacteria, thereby causing the bacteria to fluoresce green, the jellyfish's native color. Other students will work with a mutated version of the gene to create bacteria that glow blue. We'll discuss the mechanics of recombinant DNA technology and gene editing. We'll also debate the ethics of genetic modification.

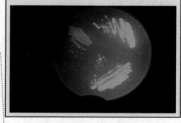

Bryan Shawn Wang July 24, 2018
Conversation among scientists, humanists, and artists, seems important, even urgent. Fortunately, in my experience, when the opportunity arises, it happens naturally.

TERRI WITEK

19. =

fever
    it
meets
    ice
deeds
    tint
seabed
    rein
city
    vulva
bans
    danced
gentle
    re
blurs
    seen

SARAH BROWN WEITZMAN

20. AMERICA, MY AMERICA

When a child I thrilled to the Anthem
and said the Pledge sincerely.
I loved the land, my hometown,
and all I knew of the rest of America.
I understood why our first settlers
came here to be free and was proud to be
from such determined people.

But because we had guns we seized the land
from those who were here before us.
Though they fought well, they lost.
I visited reservations on L.I. and
elsewhere and saw what defeat means.

Slavery for hundreds of years. *Slavery!*
Prosperity for some. Robber barons,
stock market crash, trade unions
making sweetheart contacts.
Polluted waters devoid of fish.
The earth soaked in pesticides.
Insider trading. Long lists of extinct species.

But I knew exactly who our enemies
were in WWII and understood why
we had to be at war. We gave our blood.
But afterwards things seemed to change
and war became vague and cold.

Woody Guthrie's "This Land Is Your Land"
I loved and "America the Beautiful,"
all north and south and east and west of it.

© KONINKLIJKE BRILL NV, LEIDEN, 2020 | DOI:10.1163/9789004418820_020

All the mountains and valleys and
coasts and deserts and plains.
It was more than a place to me.

Then the fight for rights despite The Bill.
What happened after I left school?
Were our ideals paper only.
Yet such great ideals.

Government despite party
change is much the same.
Now old enemies are friends
of sorts. Now on our soil
fanatics try to destroy us
from without and within.

Was my America a child's illusion,
my patriotism based on ignorance?
Was there always greed
and corruption? Have our goals
and founding principles been replaced
by the Almighty Dollar?

America, I will always love you
but who are you? the land?
the people? the government?
the leaders? the laws?
If I had to choose I would say
the land and the laws
though I once thought thunder
a thing of wonder until I heard
the **scientific explanation**.

JESSICA MOORE

21. EXPRESSIVE WRITING PARADIGM: AN EXPERIMENT IN RIGHTING

Thank you for participating in this writing study. Please follow the instructions written below over the next four days. Your writing is confidential and will not be re(a)d by anyone but you.

"Over the next four days, take 15 minutes each day to write about your deepest thoughts and emotions. Find a place where you will not be disturbed. Write continuously without interruption. Write only for yourself and don't worry about spelling or grammar. Really let go and explore. You might link your writing to the past, present, or future, or who you have been, who you are now, or who you would like to be. The only rule is that once you begin writing, continue to do so until time is up."

Day 1: Denial [#fakenews]

Take 15 minutes today to avoid all of your thoughts and emotions. If you have informed thoughts or heightened emotions, keep them to yourself because no one cares. Overburden yourself so that you will not be disturbed; stay busy. Clean and organize your disgusting home, improve the deficiencies of your body, purchase new and improved feelings. Right continuously without interruption with no consideration for your own desires. Never let go and explore. Doing so might prompt you to become aware and disrupt your psychosocial internment. Once you shut out all thoughts and emotions, continue to do so even when time is up.

Day 2: Anger [8 U.S. Code § 1531 § 18.5.19.9.19.20]

Take 15 minutes to right your deepest thoughts and emotions. Find a place where you will not be disturbed by **diversity**, solidarity, or the nationless. Right continuously without interruption. Right and don't worry about **science** or **evidence**. Let go of your desire for healthcare; you are not worthy. You might link your righting to the past, present, or future, or the **fetus** you once were, the living soul you are now, or who you would like to become as long as you are not **transgender**. Once you begin righting, continue to do so until you arrive at a wall.

Day 3: Bargaining [Writes]

Take back 15 **vulnerable** minutes to right your deepest thoughts and emotions. Find places you will disturb the status quo. Write continuously without interruption from those attempting to shut you up. Right for **diversity** and the **vulnerable**, and leverage the power of language to speak your truth. Let art and **science** be companions of comfort. You might link your writing to the past, present, or future, or who people wanted you to be, who you are now, or who you aspire to become. Once you begin resisting, the writing will become increasingly effortless as you let the rules fade away.

Day 4: Depression [ICD-10 F32.5 Full Remission]

Take as little or as much time as you want to write about your deepest thoughts and emotions. Discover places to write where you can just allow yourself to be. Write in spite of the inevitable interruption(s). Write first and foremost for yourself, but recognize the power of your words when you set them free. Let your words fly from the page into shared spaces. You might link your writing to the past, present, or future, or who we have been, who we are now, or who we are becoming. Once you begin writing, continue to do so. Time is never up. Thank you for accepting this self-study. Take a few days off and then come back to reflect on your acts of resistance.

SCOTT WIGGERMAN

22. TO BEAT THE BANNED

A gob of gel, a glob of goo,
too young to yet be a **fetus**.
I may always stay an embryo,
content with being a nucleus.

Too speculative, too **vulnerable**,
a bit of squiggle, a snick of squirm,
like many lives, I'm accidental,
the hook-up of an egg and sperm.

Not male, not female, a touch
of both, which shouldn't be a crime.
I might be **transgender** in a clutch
and create my own paradigm.

A clot, a curd of **diversity**,
I add to myself each day.
I will be what I want to be,
not what conservatives say.

A spit of this, a spot of that,
afloat in this environment.
This hydroponic habitat
exists as my **entitlement**.

Facts are always **evidence-based**
or else they wouldn't be facts,
as science is always **science-based**—
or are these just means to distract?

© KONINKLIJKE BRILL NV, LEIDEN, 2020 | DOI:10.1163/9789004418820_022

JENNIFER K. SWEENEY

23. FOUR YEARS

Every day that Obama was president I was tuned a little out, like we'd made it through the Bush years and I could slip back from the glare. Every day I was not thinking about the rise of hate groups in America, not thinking that a woman could be witch-hunted and we would watch it syndicate. Every day drinking coffee, kids toddling, every morning very tired trying to write.

Still wooed by beauty, still thinking that there is a good world out there, a general decency we could mostly recognize. When I published a poem, I posted it. When my kids said cute things, I shared. Liked. Liking dulled the thing but I kept liking. When I thought about my future, I always imagined it without social media, as if remembering the old normal and assuming the lens would eventually splinter. Relieved for that moment not of my own making that did not come.

Every day I did not cry, I never sobbed, sleeping was past-tense; civil rights, Roe v. Wade and the KKK were all past-tense. Every day that it was possible that Donald Trump could be our president, it was not possible. A joke, a reality show gone too far.

Waiting it out. First with chips and a beer. Then whiskey and heart-terror.

Even if it would never happen, this was damaging. If I watched Maddow every night, and read all the articles, and supported Hillary, if I witnessed every horrible thing and did not turn away from any of it, this would safeguard. Right up until midnight on November 8. Still safeguarding.

Every day after, I sobbed. Every day after, wrote nothing except emails to congress people and ongoing drafts of letters to Hillary Clinton in my head. Every day, Hillary Clinton eats a jalapeno, I read once in an article called "Things You Never Knew about Hillary Clinton."

I can't get this out of my head. All of it. But the jalapeno. I keep coming back to it. Not because it's a catchy snap of trivia, but because it's deeply human, purposeful, committed, a bit daring, and somewhat inconvenient. So little we allowed her. Maybe she slices it, gives it a sauté, I don't know, but I see her eating it whole, entering the howl of another day where the collective misunderstanding of her is the narrative, bearing the shock, becoming the fire.

© KONINKLIJKE BRILL NV, LEIDEN, 2020 | DOI:10.1163/9789004418820_023

My friend says I need to work on my insults, that it's too much baggage to carry around that nicey-nice mask into my 40s.

Reading my son a picture book the girl (tragically kind) asks *Is it too late to undo what has been done?*

I felt if I did not turn away it meant something like the one who will not leave the hospital bed after being told get a shower get some rest. But what if the breathing stops while I turn away? What if the heart goes emptying in its basket?

I mistype **vulnerable** as vulbearable and it seems accurate.

If I watch it, is it a vigil? An illusion? An obsession disguised as an act of prevention? Cars careening toward each other and trying to make the calls, trying to scream into the moment before.

Election, you bad boyfriend, I can't quit you, my friend writes. These unending fall months, we don't know we are watching a loss, we don't know anything.

The first acts are of negation. Policies, people, empty offices that will never be full. Words can be sheared away. ***Diversity*** and ***vulnerable***. Gone are the facts, the **evidence**, **science** swept from sites with a silent click. Entitled in his Palm Beach White House, he erases ***entitlement***.

How quickly saying "the new normal" becomes the new normal. Don't accept into the fold. Stay alert.

Is there still time? Only if watching isn't the action.

MARK KERSTETTER

24. WHILE THE OFFERING STALES IN THE CALM

What are these stentorian claims tidily stacked like Tiffany boxes against the vastness of the universe as it races out of reach of the known and knowable? Last I checked Big Bang was still in the expansion phase. We're talking about an old **fetus** here. It will not do, any longer, to enact the derisive dismissal of efforts to think past this wall by erasing the "**evidence-based**" and the "**science-based**" from its bricks. Not that we're talking about a progress of thought, just the possibility of it. *Thinking past* is not an advance but a readjustment: one reorients the arena of thought outside the wall, in the free air of expansion itself. The very possibility of becoming someone viable requires **vulnerability**. Yours. Mine. **Transgender**ed others stuck in the cracks. It goes without saying the thought units are not (or no longer) bricks. But Truth Claims were never the materials of an architecture either, just the ever shifting, ever retooling **diversity** of elements in a bricoleur's satchel as he or she concocted the precise experimentation that made up the set days of a life. How else is a star to die, lest the sky be glutted with them? But wait, don't tell me, not if your wall carries the crumbling mortar of "God," "Country" and such like, Why are you so afraid of the loose meaning on the workshop floor? Don't answer that either. I mean those bricks left the studio long ago. Nothing to be done now but let gravity have its way. Sure, a sore posterior might result, with maybe an indecorous chuckle from the gallery. But unless we subscribe to an **entitlement** that actually justifies murder we're going to be fine. And there will always be so much to ignore short of the next superstorm.

SUSAN COHEN

25. PHOTOSYNTHESIS

Another **evidence-based** day.
Not a unicorn in the sky.
I pass under a maple's **diversity**
of red, yellow, orange and brown.
Even with good intentions and a strong
work ethic, leaves are born **vulnerable**,
death being the one **entitlement**
of every living thing from blossom
to boy, from **fetus** to father.
This poem is **transgender**, meaning
surface is one thing but essence
another. It is not about trees.
We've been advised to swap words
for lies so reality will disappear.
I repeat: *vulnerable, entitlement,*
diversity, transgender, fetus,
but this maple keeps absorbing
the *evidence-based* sun
to produce *science-based* growth.
Remember photosynthesis?
Soon, someone will insist we
just call it magic so we forget
how life depends on light.

© KONINKLIJKE BRILL NV, LEIDEN, 2020 | DOI:10.1163/9789004418820_025

QUESTIONS AND ACTIVITIES FOR
FURTHER DISCUSSION

WRITING ACTIVITIES

The following writing exercises can be implemented in the classroom, in your own writing practice, or in the home as fun and educational family activities.

1. *The Acrostic.* An acrostic poem is one in which the first (or middle, or last) letter of each line spells a word to create a poem that is both a literal and visual interpretation of the said word. For a classroom exercise, break the class into seven groups and assign each group one of the seven banned words. Have each group create their own definition of the word and brainstorm examples. Next, have either the group or each individual from the group write their own acrostic poem. During the next class period, have students share what they have written. Let's take the word "**entitlement**," for example.

Endings. That one can choose to end well is
Neither chance nor a matter of minutes.
This body is able to bend, this mouth able to
Iterate a slight of hand, an injustice, a
Teaching moment of loves me or
Loves me not because I can
Entertain you with things that cost
Money and time like daisies and Air Jordans.
Educate me away from ideas like
Neutrality. Show me action. Push and
Truth me, as in how far we have not come.

2. *The RESIST Haiku.* A Haiku is a short, three-lined poem in which each line has a specific element or quality as well as a specific syllable count. The first line should communicate a season, as most Haikus communicate about the natural world. The season should not be named, but shown through imagery. This line traditionally has five syllables. The second line should be seven syllables long, and often contains a verb and a word that will serve to "cut" or juxtapose two images or ideas. The last line of a haiku is an image that we

might consider a surprise. This last line traditionally has five syllables like the first. Haikus often come in a series. For a classroom exercise, assign each student one of the seven banned words and have them write a haiku in which that word is the focal point. Then have students talk about which word they feel the poem speaks to, and why. Individual Haikus can then be put together to form a series. Here is an example using the word "**fetus**" as a focal point:

Windows burn fingers
Born to scorch and man-made floods
Heartbeat in the sand

3. Write your own poem using the banned words (**Diversity, Entitlement, Evidence-Based, Fetus Science-Based, Transgender, Vulnerable**).

Variation A. You may wish to use a poetic form, such as the Sestina, which is a poem that builds through the use of repetition around a pattern of six repeated words at the end of thirty-nine lines. See Andrea's example, *Banned Sestina*, that uses all seven banned words in the introduction.

To write a sestina: You will use the banned words as end words in six stanzas of poetry with six lines in each stanza. Decide what theme(s) you want your lines to convey using the words. You will end the poem with a three-line envoi—closing lines—that use the six words in a particular order. You will repeat the banned words as end words and in the three-line envoi in the following pattern:

- Stanza 1: A, B, C, D, E, F
- Stanza 2: F, A, E, B, D, C
- Stanza 3: C, F, D, A, B, E
- Stanza 4: E, C, B, F, A, D
- Stanza 5: D, E, A, C, F, B
- Stanza 6: B, D, F, E, C, A
- Envoi: B, E
- Envoi: D, C
- Envoi: F, A

Variation B. You may wish to write a free verse poem that incorporates some of the banned words. Try doing something like Sandra did with *Trigger Warning* in the introduction. In *Trigger Warning*, Sandra wrote a letter about guns and gun violence to the NRA (National Rifle Association), which she never sent. Sandra used the letter as source text with an online cut-up text mixing deck to generate some lines of poetry from the letter (e.g., the hunting weapon of feminist rage; find the bullets in the kitchen drawer; this shoots on a loop for years). Then Sandra wrote more lines around the generated text that resonated with the poem's themes.

To do: Begin by writing a letter to someone about something that angers you. The idea is that you are generating ideas for a poem; this letter may or may not be something you actually send. Then, use parts of the letter you wrote to compose a poem. You may wish to try an online remix generator, such as http://www.lazaruscorporation.co.uk/cutup/text-mixing-desk. Take lines from the generator that speak to the themes you wish to convey in your poem. Write other lines around them if needed.

4. Write a fictional or lyric essay about something you have not been able to write about, but have always wanted to like Jessica Smartt Gullion's "Late Term," in which Smarrt Gullion juxtaposes her own pregnancy story with the story of a woman who carried a **fetus** to term with no brain because of the politics surrounding abortion. Your essay may be about a situation that you wish you knew the resolution to. For instance, whatever happened to the young woman in your high school class who dropped out because of a pregnancy? Try using juxtaposition as a writing technique. To generate material ask yourself "What if...?"

4. Write a poem and/or brief response essay like Jennifer K. Sweeney's "Four Years" about something that makes you angry, sad, and motivated to act. Use your **entitlement** to write a response. Use your **entitlement** to weep and rage on the page. Use your writing as action and response.

5. Use Jessica Moore's satire, "Expressive Writing Paradigm: An Experiment in Righting," as a template for writing your own satire around the seven banned words. Satire can be an effective means of writing about emotional topics you feel **vulnerable** about; the use of humor as an act of resistance.

DISCUSSION QUESTIONS

1. How do the contributors in this collection use the idea of being **vulnerable** as an approach to resisting censorship in their work? What does such an approach add to creative work used for political aims? How can you use vulnerability as an approach to your creative work?

2. What does it mean to use **evidence-based practice** in creative work? How do the authors in this collection use evidence in their work? What kinds of evidence do the authors use in their work and to what effect?

3. This collection presents a **diversity** of approaches and writing techniques that authors use to talk about censorship in their work and lives. Choose your favorite piece(s) in the collection and consider what you admire in the work. What is the author doing with technique that you like? How does the author convey a compelling message?

4. In what ways do the pieces in this collection demonstrate a conversation between **science** and art? Between **scientists** and poets? What connections do the contributors make between **science** and poetic craft?

5. What benefits does a creative approach to censorship seen in the personal essays and poems in this collection provide? How is a creative approach to censorship a form of #resistance? What drawbacks are there to taking a creative approach to censorship?

NOTES ON CONTRIBUTORS

Scott M. Bade earned his Ph.D. in creative writing at Western Michigan University (WMU). In addition to teaching at Kalamazoo College and the Kalamazoo Institute of Arts, Scott is also the coordinator of the WMU Center for the Humanities. He is a former poetry editor for *Third Coast Magazine* and editorial assistant at New Issues Press. His chapbook *My Favorite Thing about Desire* was a co-winner of the 2018 Celery City Chapbook contest. His poems have appeared in *Fugue, Shadowgraph, H_NGM_N, Foothill* and elsewhere.

Lee Beavington is poet-scientist-philosopher. He is an award-winning author, educator and PhD candidate in Philosophy of Education at SFU. He has taught a wide range of courses and labs at Kwantlen Polytechnic University, including Ecology, Genetics, Expressive Arts, Advanced Molecular Biology, and the Amazon Field School, and served as co-curator for the current *Wild Things* exhibition at the Museum of Vancouver. His interdisciplinary research explores wonder in science education, environmental ethics, and arts-based learning across the curriculum. Find Lee reflecting in the forest, mesmerized by ferns, and always following the river. More about Lee at www.leebeavington.com.

Paul Bilger's photography has appeared at Qarrtsiluni, Brevity, and Kompresja. His work has also been featured on music releases by Dead Voices on Air and Autistici. When not taking pictures, he is a lecturer in philosophy and film theory at Chatham University. He is the art director at SmokeLong Quarterly. The cover image, *Stars of Eger*, was created by Paul.

Sarah Brown Weitzman, a past National Endowment for the Arts Fellow in Poetry and Pushcart Prize nominee, was a Finalist in the Academy of American Poets' Walt Whitman First Book Award contest. She is widely published in hundreds of journals and anthologies including *New Ohio Review, North American Review, The Bellingham Review, Rattle, Mid-American Review, Verse Daily, Poet Lore, Miramar, Spillway* and elsewhere. Pudding House published her chapbook, *The Forbidden*.

Michelle Bonczek Evory is the author of *Naming the Unnameable: An Approach to Poetry for New Generations* (Open SUNY Textbooks, 2018) and several chapbooks of poetry. She teaches literature at Western Michigan University and mentors poets on The Poet's Billow (www.thepoetsbillow.org).

Franklin K. R. Cline is an enrolled member of the Cherokee Nation, a PhD candidate in English—Creative Writing at the University of Milwaukee-Wisconsin, a member of Woodland Pattern Book Center's Board of Directors, and the book reviews and interviews editor of *cream city review*. His first book, *So What*, is available via Vegetarian Alcoholic Press.

Susan Cohen twice won the Science in Society award from the National Association of Science writers. A former contributing writer to the *Washington Post Magazine* and faculty member at the University of California Graduate School of Journalism, she studied poetry while on a Knight Fellowship at Stanford University and then earned an MFA from Pacific University. Her poetry honors include the Rita Dove Prize and Milton Kessler Poetry Award. She's the author of two chapbooks and two full-length collections: *Throat Singing* and *A Different Wakeful Animal,* winner of the Meadowhawk Prize from Red Dragonfly Press. www.susancohen-writer.com/

Daniela Elza's work appears nationally and internationally in over 100 publications. Her poetry collections are *the weight of dew* (Mother Tongue Publishing, 2012), *the book of It* (iCrow Publications, 2011), and *milk tooth bane bone* (Leaf Press, 2013), of which David Abram says: "Out of the ache of the present moment, Daniela Elza has crafted something spare and irresistible, an open armature for wonder." Daniela earned her doctorate in Philosophy of Education from Simon Fraser University (2011). Daniela lives and writes in Vancouver, BC.

Andrea England is the author of *Other Geographies* (2017, Creative Justice Press) and *Inventory of a Field* (Finishing Line Press, 2014). She holds an MFA and MSW from Arizona State University and received her PhD from Western Michigan University. Her work has appeared in *Midwestern Gothic, Sonora Review, The 3288 Review* and elsewhere. She lives and works between Kalamazoo and Manistee, Michigan, where she teaches English and Creative Writing for various universities and organizations.

Sandra L. Faulkner is professor of communication and Director of Women's, Gender, and Sexuality Studies at Bowling Green State University where she writes, teaches and researches about close relationships. Her interests include qualitative methodology, poetic inquiry, and the relationships among culture, identities, and sexualities in close relationships. Her latest books are *Real Women Run: Running as Feminist Embodiment* (Routledge, 2018) and *Poetic Inquiry: Craft, Method, and Practice* (Routledge, 2020). She received the 2013 Knower Outstanding Article Award from the National Communication Association for her narrative work and the 2016 Norman K. Denzin Qualitative Research Award.

Sandy Feinstein's publications include poetry set at a biology field station in Costa Rico and of a scientist at work (*XCP, Freshwater*) as well as scholarly articles on Marie Meurdrac, a seventeenth-century chemist (*Early Modern Women*), among others. She has also published creative non-fiction with no apparent connection to science (*Punctuate! & Florida English*). She coordinates the Honors Program at Penn State Berks.

Karin L. Frank, who studied to be a research neurochemist and worked as a psychologist in her youth, is an award-winning author from the Kansas City area. Her poems and prose have been published in both literary journals and genre magazines in the U.S. and abroad.

Kris Harrington writes place-infused creative non-fiction about her lifetime home, Youngstown, Ohio. She coordinates and directs *The Strand Project*, a full-length theatrical production of original dramatic monologues. A lecturer for Kent State University, Kris's work has appeared in *Dictionary of Literary Biography, The Sun, Jenny,* and *River and South Review*. She has read at YSU's *Summer Festival of the Arts*, and other local events including *Slice of Life* and *Women Artists: A Celebration*. She teaches community writing workshops and performs in local theater productions. Kris lives in Youngstown, OH, with her husband Jim, daughters Miranda and Gillian, and several rescue pets.

Elizabyth A. Hiscox is the author of *Reassurance in Negative Space* (Word Galaxy) and *Inventory from a One Hour Room* (Finishing Line). Her poetry has appeared in *DMQ Review, From the Fishouse, Gulf Coast, Hayden's Ferry Review, Matter*, and elsewhere. Former Poet-in-Residence at Durham

University (UK), she has taught writing in England, the Czech Republic, and Spain and currently instructs at Western State Colorado University where she is director of the Contemporary Writer Series and Editor-in-Chief for Western Press Books.

Mark Kerstetter is an artist and writer from St. Petersburg, Florida. He is the author of *One Step: Prayers and Curses* and blogs at The Mockingbird Sings: https://marktkerstetter.wordpress.com

Shalen Lowell is a transgender and genderfluid author, blogger, and poet from York, Maine. A trans equality advocate and activist, they specialize in fiction which represents the intersection of fantasy and postmodern genres and queer literature, as well as nonfiction work that particularly illustrates the lives, struggles, and experiences of genderfluid and nonbinary LGBTQ+ folx. Shalen's work has been published in such collections as *Privilege Through the Looking Glass*, *Massachusetts' Best Emerging Poets*, and *Challenging Genders: Non-Binary Experiences of Those Assigned Female at Birth*.

Minadora Macheret is a Ph.D. student and Teaching Fellow at the University of North Texas. She is a Poetry Editor for Devilfish Review and the Co-Coordinator of the Poets in Pajamas Reading Series. Her work has appeared in *Tinderbox Poetry Journal*, *Red Paint Hill*, *Rogue Agent*, *Connotation Press*, and elsewhere. She is the author of the chapbook, *Love Me Anyway* (Porkbelly Press, 2018). She likes to travel across the country with her beagle, Aki.

Jessica Moore Jessica Moore (Ph.D., University of Texas at Austin) is a psychotherapist in Austin, TX, and professor at St. Edward's University. Dr. Moore is a member of the International Association of Relationship Researchers, National Communication Association, and the American Association of Marriage and Family Therapists.

Ben Paulus is a poet and information architect. He studied creative writing at Beloit College in Beloit, Wisconsin, received a mentorship from the Loft Literary Center in Minneapolis, Minnesota, and was a recent finalist for the Roswell Prize for short science-fiction. His poems can be found online, and in the journal *Central Ohio Writing*. A member of the Reality Benders improv troupe, Ben lives with his son in Bend, Oregon.

Charnell Peters is a doctoral student in Communication at the University of Utah. Her work has appeared in Crab Creek Review, Apogee, Hippocampus, Fiction Southeast and elsewhere. She is the blog editor for *Ruminate Magazine*.

Jane Piirto is Trustees' Professor Emerita who worked at Ashland University. Her books on creativity and giftedness are well-known. She is an award-winning literary poet, literary novelist, and scholar in education and psychology.

Samantha Schaefer is a writer, yogi, artist, artist, and poet—born and raised in Kalamazoo, MI. She received her MFA in Poetry as a Follett Fellow at Columbia College Chicago. She has since worked as co-editor of *Black Tongue Review*, Editorial Intern at *Yoga International*, and as Writer in Residence at Brushcreek Foundation for the Arts. Nominated for two Pushcart Prizes, her poetry explores multi-modal composition, collaboration between artistic genres, and all things uncanny. Her poetry can be found in publications such as *TYPO*, *Columbia Poetry Review*, *Ghost Town Literary Magazine*, and *Caesura*.

Jessica Smartt Gullion is the Associate Dean of Research for the College of Arts and Sciences at Texas Woman's University, where she is also a tenured Associate Professor of Sociology. Her research interests include ontology, posthumanism, and qualitative methodology. Her recent books include *Diffractive Ethnography* and *Writing Ethnography*.

Jennifer K. Sweeney is the author of three poetry collections: *Little Spells* (New Issues Press, 2015), *How to Live on Bread and Music* (2009, Perugia), which received the James Laughlin Award, the Perugia Press Prize and a nomination for the Poets' Prize, and *Salt Memory* (2006, Main Street Rag). The recipient of a Pushcart Prize, her poems have recently appeared in *The Adroit Journal*, *American Poetry Review*, *The Awl*, *Cimarron Review*, *Crab Orchard*, *Kenyon Review Online*, *Love's Executive Order*, *Mississippi Review*, *New American Writing*, *Stirring*, *Terrain*, *Thrush* and *Verse Daily*.

Bryan Shawn Wang teaches biochemistry and molecular biology at Penn State Berks. He also has a long-standing interest in literature and has published fiction in *Gulf Stream*, *Potomac Review*, *Washington Square*, and *Kenyon Review Online*.

Scott Wiggerman is the author of three books of poetry, the most recent being *Leaf and Beak: Sonnets,* finalist for the Texas Institute of Letters' Helen C. Smith Memorial Award; and the editor of a dozen other books, including the best-selling *Wingbeats I & II: Exercises & Practice in Poetry* (Dos Gatos, 2014) and the anthology *Weaving the Terrain: 100-Word Southwestern Poems.* Recent poems have appeared in *Softblow, The Ghazal Page, Contemporary Haibun,* and *Allegro Poetry Magazine.* He lives in Albuquerque, New Mexico, with his husband, writer David Meischen.

Norma C. Wilson received a Ph.D. in English from the University of Oklahoma in 1978. After teaching literature and writing at the University of South Dakota for 27 years, she retired in 2005 as English Professor Emerita. Her books include *The Nature of Native American Poetry* (University of New Mexico Press, 2001); *Under the Rainbow: Poems from Mojácar* (Finishing Line Press, 2012); *Memory, Echo Words* (Scurfpea Publishing, 2014); and with visual artist Nancy Losacker, *Rivers, Wings & Sky* (Scurfpea Publishing, 2016). She and her husband Jerry Wilson live in a geo-solar house they built in rural Vermillion, South Dakota.

Terri Witek is the author of 6 books of poems, most recently *The Rape Kit*, winner of the 2017 Slope Editions Prize judged by Dawn Lundy Martin. Her work often traces the breakages between word and image. She teaches Poetry in the Expanded Field in Stetson University's MFA of the Americas, and holds the Sullivan Chair in Creative Writing.

Printed in the United States
By Bookmasters